I want to like my Garden

How to make your garden better

Rachel McCartain

THE CHOIR PRESS

Copyright © 2020 Rachel McCartain

All rights reserved. No part of this publication may be reproduced or transmitted in any form or by any means, electronic or mechanical including photocopying, recording or any information storage or retrieval system, without prior permission in writing from the publishers.

The right of Rachel McCartain to be identified as the author of this work has been asserted by her in accordance with the Copyright, Designs and Patents Act 1988

First published in the United Kingdom in 2020 by
The Choir Press

ISBN 978-1-78963-113-5

My thanks for permission to use images of their gardens to: L Pointer; A Ryman; R Currim; S Connell.

Pictures on pages 27, 103, 104, 123, 127, 128, 129, 137, 140, 141, 143, 144, 145 via pixio.com or are in the public domain and have no accredited author unless stated.

Page 13 – Vinca (Bicanski); 100 – Hanging basket (Bicanski); 145 – Tulip (Ilyessuti); 145 – Fern (Adam Pelletier); 143 – Clematis (PDD), 144 – Papaver (Pixel 2013).

All other images are copyright of Rachel McCartain and PlantPlots.

PlantPlots

Rachel doesn't just write gardening books, there's a brilliant website offering lots of advice plus loads of ready-made garden border designs available to download in an instant.

Fountains & Fluff

✓ Dancing in the breeze (the plants that is!)

✓ Poor soils & sunny sites

✗ People who like neat & tidy gardens

✗ Rich soils or damp corners

Email:
rachel@plantplots.com

Visit plantplots.com

plantplots.com the gardening website for non-expert gardeners!

Acknowledgments

Books are never written without the unfaltering support of friends and family who labour through draft after draft with unfailing attention to detail, suggesting alterations, reviewing the content and providing some much-needed moral support to keep on going.

So, thank you my friends.

Allium Hair, it's a bit odd, but I like them!

Contents

ACKNOWLEDGMENTS	iv
I WANTED MY GARDEN TO BE BETTER	1
DO YOU LIKE YOUR GARDEN?	5
What stops you enjoying the garden?	6
Putting things right	16
Learn to love your garden again	20
IMPROVING THE GARDEN	22
What's the difference between a front and back garden?	22
How to make an existing border lower maintenance	26
Proper planting	34
Perfectly good pruning	38
What to do with misbehaving plants	40
HOW TO CHANGE THE GARDEN	50
Rules to remember before you do anything!	51
Designing around problems you can't change	58
First time gardeners	63
Drawing the design	70
Planting with 'boxes'	76
Garden styles and why they don't work	79
Common garden mistakes	84

HOW YOUR GARDEN CAN HELP SAVE THE WORLD	113
OK, IT MIGHT NOT BE THE WORLD'S GREATEST GARDEN BUT …	130
USEFUL STUFF TO KNOW ABOUT PLANTS	132
Designing with 'Boxes'	146
BIBLIOGRAPHY	154
INDEX	155
AND FINALLY …	158
ABOUT THE AUTHOR	159

Books are usually dedicated to our favourite people, those we love and of course I thank them, for without them I would not, nor could not be me.

But this dedication looks to the future; and is to those not yet born, but who will have to live with the consequences of our actions today.

I only hope when they look back, the overriding sentiment is one of relief; that we really did do something to tackle climate change.

'Look deep into nature, and then you will understand everything better'

Albert Einstein

I wanted my garden to be better

I really wanted to love my garden; the problem was I didn't like gardening, but every time I stepped outside; I was just confronted with the gardening jobs that needed doing. My mood would change from pleasure to frustration; I couldn't relax and enjoy being outside as all I saw were chores and unfinished jobs, being in my garden was no fun.

Gardening is supposed to be a pleasure but more often it's not; which got me thinking, why did gardening always feel like just another chore. Why was the garden making me feel so empty and would changing the garden or how I did the gardening help make the whole experience feel more enjoyable?

Over the years I have read many books and watched countless gardening programmes on the television, but all seemed to follow the same broad approach; and focussed on how you 'do' gardening. The trouble was I didn't enjoy doing that sort of gardening, I have never propagated plants or taken cuttings, it just wasn't something that interested me. Growing seed was fine, potting small plants into bigger pots was ok, but the other aspects of gardening just weren't something I wanted to do.

In addition, the garden I had created bore little resemblance to those shown in books or on television programmes. It was not packed full of interesting and unusual plants species. I did not have special areas for succulents to grow or an Auricula theatre, there were no long borders and neither did I have a cutting garden. So, did all that mean everything I was doing wasn't really gardening? Was I to be forever consigned to the 'never mind; you tried' club of gardeners, because it's only the truly expert horticulturalists who can produce stunningly beautiful gardens?

No wonder I felt such disappointment, how on earth could I ever create a little piece of paradise when I wasn't interested in all the aspects of gardening? But I wondered was that all that gardening was; just propagating, potting on, pricking out and pruning? If so, it's no wonder I didn't enjoy it and I didn't want to be a gardener!

I still wanted my garden to be the best it could be and be a place I enjoyed spending time in. To learn to love my garden I had to understand what I loved about being in my garden and analyse why 'doing the gardening' left me feeling so deflated.

I began to realise that for me, gardening was the pleasure derived from creating an environment outside my back door, that I enjoyed managing in a way that fitted in with my life. It was about creating a place for me to feel in partnership with nature.

As such the business of gardening was only necessary if my enjoyment of the space was affected by something. So, I only needed to prune if a plant got in the way, I didn't need the flowers to look perfect, I just wanted them to look good. The result was that the act of gardening became less demanding, the garden performed to my set of standards.

Gardening is not a scientific discipline; gardens merely show the level of love their owner has for them. Consequently, there can be no good gardeners or bad gardeners; only those in love or out of love with their gardens. If you are unhappy with your garden, it's not because you aren't an expert or aren't very good at gardening, it's because you are just not in love with your garden. Which is why I have written this book, to show how you can have a garden you love, if like me, you don't want to learn how to be a gardener.

This book doesn't include 'the business' of horticulture (the technical stuff, like pruning, grafting, lifting or dividing and so forth) primarily as there is an ocean of information out there already, but more importantly because those skills are only needed if you want to be a proper gardener; but if you don't want to become one, why would you want to learn them?

This book is split into three sections; understanding why your garden is not working; showing you how to make changes that will improve the garden and finally how your gardening methods can also help save the world.

The last section is the most important and is my most passionately held belief about gardening; which is that gardens should not just look good, they should do good too.

Gardens are not separate from nature; they are part of nature, how we all garden makes a difference to the wellbeing of our planet and to the health of future generations.

If by reading this book, how you garden becomes as important as the garden; I will be delighted.

Gardens aren't just for us

Do you like your garden?

Gardening has been one of this nation's favourite pastimes and collectively we lavish billions on our gardens every year. Over the last decade, there has been a resurgence in interest, attendance at flowers shows is at an all-time high as new and first-time gardeners begin to learn the art of the garden. Despite all this interest though, many households are reluctant to call themselves gardeners; and don't find owning a garden much of a pleasure. Although these gardens are usually mowed and tended, they are unloved and underperforming spaces, the owner does not like either gardening or does not like the garden itself.

'Happy' flowers, always a good bet!

If this book is to help you love your garden a little more, why it fell out of favour in the first place needs to be addressed.

Gardens evolve over time; plants ebb and flow with the changing seasons and how we use our gardens throughout our lives changes too. Gardens may transform from purely adult spaces to external playgrounds before transforming back again later. Each time period requires the garden to shift focus, to ensure it remains both a useful and enjoyable place to be. The garden's lifespan then, should mirror your own, but there may be times when your life and that of your garden fall out of synch and it becomes a place you derive little pleasure from. Gardens are places we should all enjoy using, they should evoke positive emotions and fill the senses with sights and sounds, movement and scent; but you cannot love your garden if the only emotion provided is a negative one. Analysing which factors and elements prevent you from enjoying the garden is essential; if you don't know exactly what's wrong, you can never put it right.

If the garden offers little bar being space outside; you are unlikely to enjoy being in it.

Less negatives mean more positives, you may not love gardening, but at least you may learn to dislike it less.

Gardens fail for three reasons, you can't use them how you would like to, the plants that grow aren't suitable for the space and the garden fails to tick any emotional boxes; it just leaves you feeling flat. The road to redemption then is threefold but involves asking some non-horticultural questions.

What stops you enjoying the garden?

The most important point to establish is what it is that prevents you from enjoying the garden as you would wish to. There will be many possible reasons why, but the key here is you. The question is why you can't enjoy the garden and not what is wrong with the garden. Some of the reasons will be structural, some environmental and some emotional, but you need to look at each one and work out whether you can make a change to the garden itself or whether you need to find a solution that bypasses the problem. The sorts of issues that might arise include:

- Noise; either neighbours or traffic or both.
- The shed has been built in the best part of the garden.
- Privacy; there is nowhere to sit without being overlooked.

Do your like your garden?

* Or there is nowhere to sit at all.
* Or maybe it doesn't feel like a garden at all, it is just a space surrounded by fences.

Once you have your list of reasons, assign one of three causes to each problem, either structural, environmental, or emotional; as this identifies the primary route needing to be taken to resolve the problem, so for example this list of issues could read something like this:

Noise is an environmental problem, you can't affect the cause, you need to find a route around the problem. Maybe installing a water feature will help distract your attention or perhaps planting can be used that creates a nice sound when the wind blows.

The Shed clearly is a structural problem, it has hijacked the best sunbathing spot. It will need moving elsewhere.

Privacy is however an emotional problem; you can't enjoy the garden because something feels wrong. Emotional problems may need structural and or environmental solutions. Where are you being overlooked from and can anything be placed there to stop that? In addition, what changes to the planting style will help you feel more relaxed in the garden?

Not having anywhere to sit is structural, you need to identify the nicest parts of the garden where you enjoy sitting most and form a plan so you can get there and sit comfortably.

The garden not feeling much like a garden is an emotional problem, the garden is just not pushing any of your enjoyment or relaxation buttons. The first step here is for you to decide what those buttons are. If you can

Cotinus Coggyria shining in the winter sunshine.

change or amend something so you dislike it less, you end up liking it more!

Pushing your 'garden buttons'

Gardens should make you feel something, but that shouldn't be boredom, frustration or stress. Dealing with the causes of the structural and environmental issues your garden faces will remove many of the negative feelings the garden creates, but for your garden to become more enjoyable, you need to add in some positive feelings. Our emotions are stimulated by all our senses and plants can be very good at making us feel emotional. They do this by filling the air with a perfumed scent and who doesn't like running their fingers through soft tactile leaves or grasping the scent of lavender flowers? It is however important to work any design around what you want to do in the garden, the design and planting should complement those activities, because then the design works with you creating a positive relationship.

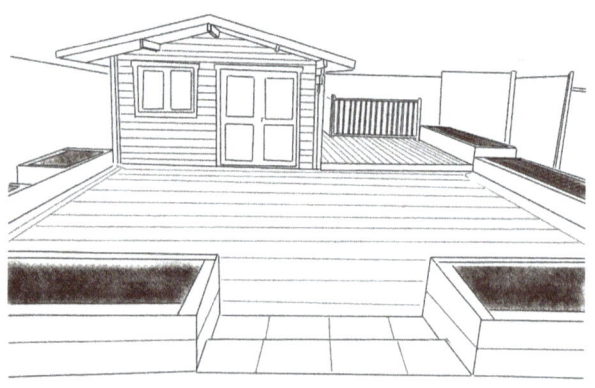

Take this summerhouse with a large decked area, it has space for a large BBQ but is surrounded with large (yet unplanted) raised borders. Clearly this will become a well-used part of the garden, a place where a family spends time together; it will be a happy place. The planting then should reflect how that space will be used.

A planting scheme that consisted of dense green hedges or formal rose bushes would seem out of place. A more appropriate style would be to use plants that were tactile, with bright happy colours and a nice scent.

Ideally, these should also be plants that attract butterflies and foraging insects, as this would help make this family space more enjoyable for adults and children alike.

Deciding what plants to put in any garden is always the trickiest part especially for those who aren't plant experts, how would you know what to plant in a border if you don't know the names of many plants; it is an impossible task. Consequently many garden owners 'play safe' with the plants they choose because they don't want to make a mistake and get it wrong, the result is a garden that does nothing for them, it simply exists. If the plants in a garden give nothing to you, the garden becomes no more than a space outside.

The plants you have in your garden should have emotional labels attached to them. The plant may have been a gift, or you may have bought a plant because it reminded you of a place you visited. It doesn't matter what the reason is, you will have a stronger emotional connection with your garden and that makes you feel better.

Does your garden provide you with positive emotions?

One method I have used over several years is to always choose plants by how I want to feel when I look at them in a border. So, for example if it's a bright and happy feel or a soothing quiet space that's needed, searching for plants in the garden centre simply involves walking up and down the aisles looking for a plant that evokes those feelings. It won't matter that you didn't know a Helenium existed, but having passed one on the shelf, if the flower put a smile on your face then you know it will be right for the border.

Now obviously there are other factors that need to be considered as well, but this method is a good starting point. If you are planning to create a new border or redesign the garden, you can easily compile a list of suitable plants that hit your emotional spot.

You will have created a mood board list of plants that all create the right feeling for the border, combining them is then a matter of using the boxes system which is described later in the book to put the border together.

Planting a problem

Gardening faux pas occur all the time and no one is immune to the odd mistake. Having planted the seemingly perfect specimen in the border, it will begin to follow one of four different paths:

- It grows beautifully and looks like the image on the label. A thumbs up then.
- It grows but never looks that good, so was probably planted in the wrong place.
- It grows everywhere; and just is wholly unsuitable for the garden.
- It makes a valiant attempt at surviving but fails.

If the plant is in the right place, it grows better and needs less looking after

Do your like your garden?

Plants are sold as instant fixes for the garden; the trouble is they aren't!

Plants grow best if they are happy where they are growing, if they aren't happy, they misbehave. Reducing the unnecessary work caused by poor planting improves how you feel about your garden instantly. Just like indoors, if the layout of the furniture in the room is not working, you shift it around, do the same in the garden. Move plants that are struggling into places they will like growing.

There is however one other reason why the plants misbehave, and it has nothing to do with you or the garden, it is down to how it was grown.

Gardening has changed in the last twenty years and unfortunately now relies far more on instant effect. Visits to garden centres have evolved from places to source plants to places where plants are now actively marketed and sold.

Garden centres showcase plants in prominent displays all selling the 'instant garden'. Trolley next to trolley are laden with pre-planted pots, hanging basket displays, plants that are smothered in oddly coloured flowers, miniature herb gardens and so forth. The displays are colourful and adorned with enticing 'buy me now' offers, and many customers do just that. The problem with instant gardening and having this supermarket selling approach to plants is that the most fundamental question is never asked by the consumer. It is a question which if not answered causes gardening disappointment, unnecessary work, is wasteful and expensive; the question:

Why would I need this plant?

Architectural it maybe; but those points will be a pain in the bottom!

If you buy on impulse it is less likely your purchase will have any beneficial impact. Buying plants is expensive, it is better to be a little more considered when spending money; are the plants you wish to buy being bought for the right reason and have a purpose? Answering this one simple question ensures you will not have spent money buying a possible problem, you will know you have spent money creating a benefit.

So, it is fine to be attracted to the 'oh that's pretty' display aisle, but before it goes in the trolley, ask a few questions.

- Where will I put it?
- Will it still fit in five years' time?
- Is it likely to survive for a full five years, if not why am I buying it?
- Will this plant do what I want it to do?
- Aside from a looking attractive, what else will this plant do for the garden?

If you are happy with the answers, buy the plant, you have justified its place in the garden.

Plants have evolved to grow in every conceivable climate and environment, if we try to grow them in an environment for which they are not suited; things quickly go wrong. Planting them in the right place ensures the plants do what they naturally want to do, and they will look after themselves, which means you don't have to!

Plants have a dark side too

I have been gardening for over 30 years now and have acquired a plethora of books and articles on all aspects of gardening, but I have yet to come across any publication that deals with the darker side of the plants available to buy. We are only ever shown glossy pictures of the flowers and foliage and details on where to plant, but never do we see anything on a plant label that says: 'don't plant here because it will ...' or 'this plant spreads faster than a viral tweet – beware where you plant!'

Now obviously the plant retailers are not going to advertise any downside, they want to sell that plant, but the gardening media don't mention this either. There is absolutely nothing wrong with extolling the virtues of a plant, but equally important is knowing where not to plant something.

A classic case in point is Vinca, which is a very pretty plant with pale blue flowers and leaves. The RHS website's plant description of Vinca is as follows;

'V. major is a vigorous evergreen sub-shrub forming a clump of erect stems bearing glossy ovate leaves and solitary violet-blue flowers 4cm wide in the leaf axils, with long rooting sterile stems making effective ground cover.'

But this is what V. major does ...

V. major is a very vigorous low growing plant. It is however pretty, with pale blue flowers and oval shaped leaves. It is best grown in shady places under trees where other plants struggle to grow, where it will happily cover the ground and smother weeds. It should never be planted in a sunny garden border; this is a plant that will quickly smother other plants given the right growing conditions. If you want it in your garden, plant it in a pot and don't let it escape.

Vinca, a plant with a 'dark' side.

Which plant description is more informative, especially for novice gardeners? Telling why and where not to plant, will not stop customers buying plants; it will only prevent customers buying unsuitable plants.

Without this vital information is it any surprise when wholly inappropriate plants are shoehorned into spaces they will outgrow within weeks. The onus for preventing a plant thug taking over the garden is sadly placed firmly on the shoulders of an unsuspecting albeit well intentioned gardener. (See Plants that fight back page 135).

Plan for debris

All gardens create mess and dealing with this mess takes time and effort, consequently all gardeners need to plan for debris, but very few do.

Knowing which plants are messy or untidy or produce loads of annual growth is important, if you want to create a garden that won't constantly demand attention.

All gardeners need to plan for debris, but very few do

It's not just your garden that can affect the level of debris, what your neighbour plants can directly impact your garden space too, which makes being a considerate gardener important. You don't want to be shovelling up debris the neighbour's trees dropped over your fence and nor do your neighbours want to deal with the wind-blown detritus from your garden. Knowing how much mess a plant, tree or shrub makes is and should be a consideration for everyone; so, what constitutes mess?

- Falling debris; leaves, twigs, seeds, fruit, berries; you wouldn't plant a tree whose dropping fruits create stains, above a wooden decking or a white stone patio for example.
- Big leaves; how do they rot down, can these be easily raked up, do they quickly form a green/brown slimy residue?
- Will the fruit rot on the tree or shrub if it's not removed, encouraging wasps?
- Will the tree drop 'bombs' of cones or seed pods or overripe fruit?
- How many seeds will form, how prolific a self-seeding plant is this; buy one get ten thousand free?

Choosing a plant for the garden is not just about right plant, right place, consideration needs to be given to how much additional or unnecessary work will be created where it is planted. For example, decorative stone mulches; it is impossible to rake or blow leaves from stone mulches (excluding pea shingle), all the leaves require picking out by hand. You cannot easily rake pine needles from any shingle either; I know that problem all too well! In addition, how easy is it dispose of garden debris and detritus. If these things are not thought through, a whole load of unnecessary work will be added to the list of garden chores.

There is a list of some of the worst offenders in the Messy Trees and Untidy Plants category at the back of the book.

Putting things right

If the garden no longer suits you or it can't be used easily, changes are required, but where to start if the list of changes needed is long? In not being a particularly enthusiastic

Maximum reward for minimal effort equals a happier gardener

gardener, you are less likely to have 'doing the garden' high up your list of domestic activities to juggle, which means you need to learn to get the most out of the time you have available.

Prioritise the changes and rank them in terms of their effort: reward ratio. Those jobs where the improvement to the garden far outweighs the effort in making the change, are the jobs you tackle first. This helps you build up momentum. If in the time you have available, the work done to change the garden has had real impact and produced improvements, you will begin enjoying the garden more. The problems that prevented you using the garden the way you want will be disappearing, the garden automatically feels less like a chore. It opens the possibility you may begin to enjoy 'doing the garden', because it no longer means constantly dealing with those chores you dislike so much.

Boring gardens aren't designed they evolve

This is 'safe' but dull.

Gardens are supposed to evoke feelings when we use them, but what if sitting in your garden just leaves you feeling a bit flat? The garden is not delivering something, you don't feel anything positive using the space, so why? Several symptoms come into play here, but the key cause is simply the garden doesn't 'do' anything. It plods along

Do your like your garden?   17

Make your garden interesting, unleash your creativeness! This is Eric the Heron, which I made from leftover chicken wire.

from season to season always looking the same; you cannot look forward to anything, because nothing ever happens.

None of us would ever go about actively creating a boring space to be in, the boringness creeps in under the radar little by little so you don't see it coming. Plants that may once have been spectacular but were short lived have been replaced with more reliable but less showy varieties. The effort you made to create displays of flowers all year have been side-lined because you just hadn't had time to do them.

It's not that you don't want a lovely garden, it's just that life has got in the way; you have had to adapt the garden to suit your needs, but unfortunately those changes have created a dull and uninspiring place. The garden simply exists, it is time to reinvigorate and make some changes, but what and how?

There was a time in our youth when fashion was important, we spent time and money getting 'the look' just right, we committed to that effort because we had few real responsibilities and it was all worth it. Gradually over time, making the effort became less important because it ate into the time available to do activities we wanted to.

The immaculate look was gradually replaced with a smart casual style that was easier to maintain and eventually by the time middle age crept up, comfort and practicality had taken over. We had ditched the platform heels in favour of Birkenstocks and could now only gaze at photos of our former selves remembering when we had the time available to purely devote to looking a million dollars. In terms of the garden then, this is the dilemma, how can you create a garden knowing that more interesting gardens require time and effort; when you don't have the time. Wouldn't it be fantastic if there was a method that wouldn't require too much time and effort; in other words, is there the gardening equivalent of the little black dress!

Well, sadly there isn't any plant by itself that could take the place of the ubiquitous black dress, but you can remodel the garden easily and it starts with sorting through your wardrobe of plants.

Reworking the garden wardrobe

What on earth is your garden wardrobe you may well ask? It's a very useful analogy to help understand how the plants in the garden and the design of the garden work together.

Plant buying is expensive, so I am not advocating you hot foot it to the nearest plant nursery, credit card in hand and purchase some

This is all jeans and jumpers …

wonder plants to reinvigorate the garden, instead the first step is to look at the 'wardrobe' in the garden right now and coordinate the contents better. It's time to create some new outfits and learn how to show them off.

Having looked at what is in the garden, it may be the wardrobe is not well balanced, there are too many jeans, jackets and jumpers or maybe there are so many different shapes, colours and styles of accessory; it all looks a mess. As to the underwear, well you'll need to decide if your style is more Bridget Jones; dependable reliable but a bit restrictive or you are more of a boxer's fan; loose and free to move but prone to falling out (sorry) over!

… whereas although colourful, these are all just accessories.

If the garden has become uninspiring and dull, change does not automatically mean a complete makeover or digging the garden up and starting afresh.

Tops and T-shirts	*These are the plants that create different outfits over the seasons*	*Perennials that flower at different times of the year or plants with colourful foliage*
Accessories	*Items that finish the look*	*Bulbs, showy flowers, and any garden accessories you add in, like gnomes for example*
Underwear	*These are the parts of the garden that aren't noticeable, but help hold everything in place*	*Border shapes and sizes, the pots used in the garden, materials used, and garden furniture*
Jeans and Jumpers	*The 'clothes' the garden wears all the time, that are comfortable, timeless and dependable*	*Most usually shrubs, trees and evergreens. All are reliable performers*

We don't throw all our old clothes out just because we are bored with them, we combine clothes differently to create new outfits. It may mean buying a new item of clothing so we can create a whole series of new looks, but the important point is that it is the process of changing things around that creates the interest.

- Move plants around to create a new look.
- Review your colour themes. Are there too many different colours all over the place?
- Concentrate your efforts; having one amazing border display is better than several little bitty ones.
- Change the shape of the lawn but there are some lawn rules to follow (see lawn rules page 103).

* Explore your senses; every plant should tick at least two or three sensory boxes, sight, smell, taste, touch or sound.

* And why not challenge convention; who said lawns must be a uniform height, shrubs don't need to be shaped into giant domes and why do hedges need to be straight and level.

Learn to love your garden again

Having a garden should be one of life's pleasures, but it can all too easily not be, which is a shame. Too many gardens are underused and unloved, not because the owner dislikes having a garden; it's just that the owner and garden have nothing in common. The first step to improving any garden then is to work out why it is not meeting your requirements, identifying what elements of the garden prevent you from enjoying the space as you want to and then taking steps to remedy those faults.

The key to learning to enjoy your garden is then to begin to start to make positive changes in the garden, these changes will have a purpose, which is to make your life better, as such the effort required to make the change becomes worthwhile. If all the jobs in the garden are just the gardening equivalent of cleaning the toilets or washing the floors, is it any surprise you don't like gardening?

Positive change will always have a positive outcome, you will benefit from the improvements in the garden and you will most likely use the garden more as a result. You will have created a better garden for yourself simply by making the garden work better for you and it still hasn't mattered that you don't know how to prune properly.

To learn to love your garden more:

- Identify why YOU don't like the garden.
- Change the problems that can be changed.
- Find a solution to mitigate those problems you can't change.
- Move misbehaving plants or get rid of them.
- Use plants that change your mood.
- Rework your plant wardrobe.
- Plan for debris.

Dianthus 'Sooty' in case you were wondering.

Improving the garden

It would be wonderful if we were all able to create the perfect garden with our first attempt, but sadly this is rather wishful thinking. Aside from the fact that the garden needs to evolve to suit our changing requirements, plants also have a habit of growing the wrong way or too big or they just die; meaning the garden changes itself and those changes may not be what we want. Consequently, the garden will always need work doing to it, change will always need to be made but how do we decide what those changes need to be? How can you decide if the changes you intend to make will improve the garden and not make it worse?

The starting point is to understand what the garden needs to do and then decide if it is succeeding, but most households have not one but two gardens. Improving the front or the back garden requires a slightly different thought process, the front garden is not a smaller sized back garden, you need to understand the differing roles of both gardens before you begin to think about making any changes.

What's the difference between a front and a back garden?

Aside from the blindingly obvious, front and back gardens have very different roles to play. Plants that are great for the back garden often don't work as well in the front garden, it's all to do with purpose and knowing what you are planting a specific plant for. Most design effort is usually given to 'doing' the back garden, the front garden often is planted with leftovers and ends up as just a more concentrated version of the back garden. Although this is not automatically a problem, simply shoehorning leftover plants into the front garden mimicking the layout in the back often creates a whole load of unnecessary work. The front garden operates under another set of gardening rules.

What should a front garden 'do'

Front gardens are a portal, an interface between the outside world and your own world. The walk from the car to the front door or up the garden path is the transition between these two worlds. It also makes a statement about the type of person that lives behind the front door; which may seem a melodramatic description of the front garden, but only invited guests see the back garden, the world at large sees the front.

The front needs to be a far more practical and functional space than the back garden, there are some inescapable design elements that are required universally; mess these up and the front garden can become a right pain in the 'proverbials'.

* The path to the front door MUST be the most obvious route or people will cut corners.

* Access from the drive to the door must be simple, easy and not obstructed in any way.

* Your plants should never attack you or your guests, so no spikes, thorns or 'trip me up' tendrils.

Secondary to these essentials, are some desirable elements too.

* You spend less time in the front, so it must contain more self-sufficient plants.

* It should lead people to your door and be welcoming.

* It should make you feel happy every time you get home.

This ticks all the first three rules, but would it really fill you with joy when you got home?

A good front garden should not create unnecessary work, if yours does, you need to identify which elements are causing the problem and decide how to eliminate or reduce their effects.

Size plays a part in increasing maintenance time, smaller spaces have disproportionately intense maintenance problems, mowing tiny lawns is fiddly, plants outgrow their allotted space more often and plant debris such as fallen leaves are more noticeable in small areas.

The simplest way to create or change a front garden is to first decide what it must not do and what you want to avoid and then list two or three key things the garden needs to do. The list could look something like this;

* Plants must not block the sunshine into the bay window (so there is a maximum height the plants should grow to).

* Everyone stares into the porch window (what can be strategically placed to prevent that).

* When parking the car, the gate post is always in the way; a design change is required.

* The path needs to be wide enough, to not keep accidentally stepping on the grass again, a design change would be needed.

* The front door is bright blue; all the flowers should complement the door colour.

Front gardens say a lot about who lives behind the front door!

There are no rules that require front gardens to have lawns either; grass is used as a walking and sitting-on medium, but if you never walk in the front garden, why create a lawn?

Regarding the front garden as an afterthought and not considering how it needs to function often creates a dull boring façade to your home or creates a garden that never seems to look it's best. A little planning can go a long way!

What should a back garden 'do'

Having described the front garden as a functional practical place, the role of the rear garden is less constrained, it is your space to mould and adapt to suit you. The garden becomes your own personal painting canvas that awaits the brush strokes and paint colours of your choice. Like any piece of artwork, its success is entirely subjective, some may like what's created, others won't; what matters though is whether you like the 'painting' you have created.

There are some functional requirements for a back garden to work well however but thankfully there are relatively few.

You will normally need the following:

The primary role for any back garden is to exclude as much of the outside world as possible whilst including as much of the natural world as desired

* A place to sit.
* A way to get to the place you'd like to sit.
* A place to hang the washing (with easy access).
* A place to store all the stuff that goes with having and maintaining a garden.

You may also need:

* A space large enough for little people to run around without crashing into things.
* A place for storing bins.

Everything else is subjective, the importance of each included element depends on how you want to use the garden, as are the changes needed to ensure the garden delivers what you want.

You can now start to improve how the garden works for you by making those changes you know will enhance your enjoyment of the garden. Don't forget, the aim is to make doing the gardening easier, so you have more time to enjoy being in the garden.

How to make an existing border lower maintenance

Lowering the maintenance in any garden border requires a little planning. The aim is to match the way the plant naturally wants to grow with the space the plant has available to grow; if the plant can 'do its thing' without being impeded in any way, it will grow without the extra help from you. All gardens will require some maintenance, the key to getting a low maintenance garden border is to identify those chores that create the unnecessary work and then find alternatives.

Use a colour coding scheme of maintenance needs and can then apply that to any part of the garden. Use a traffic light system to identify those areas that cause the most work and those that create the least. The aim being to create a garden with only a few red flags and more green ones.

Improving the garden 27

Once the areas have been flagged up, reducing the unnecessary maintenance involves deciding which of these orange and red flags you want to eliminate. This does not automatically mean getting rid of the culprit, changes can also lower the workload, simply moving a pot to a shadier position may mean less watering for example.

Above and below

What is above a plant and below it impacts how the plant will grow, so the amount of light it receives and the volume of nutrients it draws from the soil need to suit the plant that is grown there.

Plants grow best if they are happy with the conditions, sun lovers will be limp and feeble if stuffed in a shady corner and similarly plants that love a rich moist soil will look decidedly hungover if planted in a sun trap. All of which mean you tend them more often, they die, or you spend time and effort curtailing the overgrowth.

Happy stipa grass ...

Unhappy plants will never look good planted in the wrong place.

Having said that, some plants will go on the rampage if you plant them in perfect conditions and so are best avoided. These tough plants do have a place, but generally you only plant them where weeds are currently thriving and then they are brilliant.

The upshot is this; if you get the conditions right for the plant, it will grow more strongly, it will grow into the shape it's supposed to be and at the right speed. The stems will be less floppy, and it will produce better flowers.

Don't pack too much in

Normal gardening convention dislikes bare soil, gaps are places weeds will grow resulting in the horticultural trade advertising plants as 'gap-fillers'; the inference being the garden border must always appear full; really, why?

The aim is the plants will look after themselves, which means you don't have to!

A gap between plants only exists for a short time, that gap may be required for the plants either side to grow into. If for example, the border is only 2m square, then you need to select plants that over time will fill up that 2m square. Filling these gaps in quickly creates a border that is fit to burst; none of the plants grow as well as they should; they are all fighting each other for space, light and resources. The better approach is patience and allow the plant some space, it will then repay that good deed by growing better and require less attention; so, you don't have to spend so much time gardening.

If you would prefer visibly less soil, use bulbs; especially small plants like Crocus, Snowdrops, Alliums and Narcissus. These are narrow plants that don't fill the ground space too much or consume the goodness of the soil, but do fill the air above with colour before disappearing, leaving plenty of room for the rest of the plants to grow.

If it's already full at the start, how can the plants grow?

Reducing the chores

It is easy to create unnecessary work in any garden, so minimising the amount of work each plant choice makes is essential if you are to enjoy your garden more. The ideal for many garden owners is to have as low maintenance a garden as possible, so is there a design formula you can use to create one? Well strictly speaking no; because designing a low maintenance garden is all about understanding what YOU need your garden to do.

Gardening is only ever a chore if you end up doing stuff you don't like doing. Consequently, no two low maintenance gardens then will ever be the same. In order to create the best garden for you; start by working out what you don't like doing and find ways to minimise those elements.

Chores are only jobs you don't want to do, so identifying the worst chores and finding ways to reduce them automatically lowers your garden maintenance.

No garden will ever be maintenance free, but some aspects of gardening create more than their fair share of chores; ideally then any lower maintenance garden should limit these elements or at least minimise their effects. The most common time-consuming chores in any garden are:

* Clipping and pruning.
* Tying things in or stopping plants flopping.
* Weeding.
* Watering.
* Deadheading.
* Stopping one plant taking over the border.
* Digging up unwanted seedlings.
* Clearing away debris.
* And the most time-consuming part of all; mowing and edging the lawn.

> *Garden jobs I really dislike doing!!*
>
> Sweeping up leaves.
> Raking stones.
> Tying up up floppy plants.
> Weeding seedlings from the patio.
> Pruning prickly roses.

Creating a list of dislikes is a better way to start planning any garden border. Having sorted your 'jobs you dislike' list the next task is to determine how the plants in the garden are behaving (or not) to see which plants should stay.

Some plants will always need more attention than others, in some cases it is because of how and where the plant is growing that is the problem; the solution being to move it.

Shrubs

* Use evergreen shrubs.

* Avoid thorns!

* Check the size in five years, if it will be 10ft tall in five years, then it grows fast and will need constant trimming.

* If the diameter of the plant will be 80cm for example, plant it at least 40 cm away from a wall or fence, then the plant grows more upright and is less prone to flopping.

* Don't squash shrubs into tight spaces, like trousers that are too small; you'll end up with a 'muffin-top' that flops out over everything else.

Plants can't grow well if they constantly compete with each other.

Climbers

* Use self-clinging ones, so you don't have to constantly tie in tendrils.

* Make sure the trellis is big and sturdy enough. A plant won't get to the end of your trellis and stop; it will keep on growing and flop.

* Hang the trellis onto a bracket attached to the wall. This leaves space for growth and you can lift the trellis off the wall if you need to.

* Don't mix different climbers on the same trellis, unless one is an annual that will die after only one season.

Schizophragma supports itself, but it can get quite big.

* Plant a climber in a space that fits the ultimate size. Montana Clematis for example will swamp most garden trellis or arches in a very short time.

Plants

* Keep bedding and annual plants to a minimum.
* Avoid overbred flowers or overly large flowers, they generally require lots of food and water to keep producing the size and quantity of flower.
* Use bulbs rather than bedding plants to fill up gaps in the borders.
* Look for an AGM medal on the plant label, it will be a good performer and have better disease resistance.
* Avoid tender perennials as these will need protection to stay alive in winter.

Pots

* Use larger pots; small ones dry out too easily.
* In sunny spots use water retaining granules in the soil.
* Use a mixture of topsoil and compost, plants grow better in real soil.

Metal pots in sunny spots are a recipe for unhappy plants.

* Raise the pots off the ground to help with drainage.
* Have a pot collection in one place, watering is quicker.
* Mix slow release fertiliser into the soil mix, then it's done, and you won't have to remember to liquid feed every week. Keep the pots

well-watered though; this type of fertiliser needs water to dissolve into the soil.

The Ground

* Weed properly, simply pulling off the weed leaves will not kill the weed, you need to dig them out.
* If the soil is poor and you don't want to add lots of compost or manure, then choose plants that thrive in tough places or those that have shallow root systems like grasses that won't need much extra food.
* Bare soil around plants is fine, if you pack too much in, then all the plants compete for light, space, and food and only the toughest (usually the weeds) win. Give your plants space to get going. Any weed seeds are easy to see and quick to remove.
* Don't let anything set seed unless you want more of them, one plant can set thousands of seeds, weeds throw out millions, snip off seed heads before they ripen.

Think 5P's; Proper Preparation Prevents Poor Performance.

Proper planting

You cannot create or maintain a garden without at some point putting either plants in the ground or in pots. If a plant is planted well it is more likely to grow well and perform how you expect it to, so here is a quick guide to proper planting.

Sorting the soil

What your plant grows in is important so there are a couple of things you need to sort out before you pop any plant in the ground.

Do the trowel test; if the soil is so hard you cannot push a trowel into the soil, how do you expect a tiny root to push its way through? Make sure the hole is bigger than the pot so once it's planted, there is soft soil surrounding the roots allowing them to grow into this softer soil.

A properly prepared bed the plants will love to grow in.

Look at the soil first; what do you see? If there are no insects in the soil and it is pale or is full of stones, it is most likely a poor-quality soil, which is fine if the plant being used copes with poor soil. If the plant needs a rich soil, firstly ask should you plant it in this spot anyway, but if you do want to, then add plenty of manure or compost to the soil before you backfill around the plant. Plants need something to eat to grow well.

Water in the hole first; there are two reasons for this, firstly filling the soil with water and letting it drain away will provide the new plant with easy access to moisture. Secondly it is done to see how well the soil drains, if quickly you know you need to water the plants more especially in dry weather, if it stays in the bottom of the hole, you will need to add some grit to the base of the hole so the roots don't sit in a cold puddle after every rainfall.

Planting in a border

Putting plants in the ground is a fairly simple process, it involves digging a hole large enough for the plant and its root ball to fit in, back filling with soil, firming in and watering. And that is really it, but there are one or two tips that will help ensure the plant gets off to the best start.

* Don't let the roots dry out before you plant. Sort the soil first, then take the plant out of its pot so the roots are exposed to sunlight for as short a time as possible.
* Firm the soil around the new plant well, or the wind will cause the plant to rock about in the hole which damages the roots.
* In most cases make sure the plant is replanted to the same depth as it was in the pot, which means you should not see roots above the surface or bury the main stem of the plant under the soil. There are some plants that do need planting deeper, Clematis being the most common.
* Once it's planted water it again, this helps the soil settle around the plant as well as giving it another drink.
* Lastly, for the first year, don't let the plant dry out.

Planting larger trees or shrubs

The same rules apply as above but there are two additions.

* Larger plants have most likely been in a pot for longer, causing the roots to circle round inside the pot. These need gently teasing out and setting free before planting. This allows the new roots to find the new soil quickly, otherwise they will just keep growing round in a circle.

Large leaves and or big flowers means the plant will have an appetite.

✳ Larger plants often need staking too, this is because the wind will rock them even more easily, so the plant needs something to hold onto until it gets established. If possible, bang the stake in at 45 degrees to the soil and tie the base of the stem to the stake, rather than at top of the stem.

Finally, don't expect to see the plant sprout forth and begin growing straight away; before the plant can grow it needs to sort the root system out. It will be growing underground before you see it growing above ground.

Should you enrich the soil or not?

No plant transplants itself in the wild, so the act of pot growing and replanting is inherently unnatural for any plant, consequently, most will benefit if you add a little manure or fertiliser to the soil before filling the hole back in. It just provides a bit of easy food whilst the plant re-establishes itself. There are some plants that don't need any soil enrichment at all though, the addition of which will cause the plant to grow 'fat and flabby'. These in the main are all those plants that thrive in hot dry sunny conditions or poor soil; grasses being a good example, so check the label and see what it recommends before planting.

Planting in pots

Any plant in a pot is growing unnaturally, simply because the roots of the plant are above ground. Now they may be tucked away under the soil, but the pot is surrounded by air, so the plants are cooled and heated far more than they would be in the ground.

Pots don't always have to be filled with flowering plants to look amazing!

Plants in pots die for three main reasons:

* The roots dry out completely or can be cooked or frozen by the air temperature.
* The roots drown because water can't drain away properly.
* The plant starves to death as the level of nutrition in the compost gets used up.

Consequently, if planting into a pot these three issues need some forethought, or you will end up with a dead plant.

Rules to Remember:

* Bigger pots retain more moisture than smaller pots, they need more water but a little less often.
* Thin skinned pots especially metal ones, will cook the soil in summer and freeze the roots in winter, killing the plant. These pots need lining with an insulating material.
* Narrow necked pots prevent the plant being repotted, the pot needs smashing to get the plant out.
* The pot does not need soil all the way to the bottom if the plant has shallow roots (like a grass or an annual plant), save money and aid drainage by filling the pot with ballast first.
* After a couple of years, check the drainage holes haven't been filled with roots.
* Every year remove some of the soil and replace with new topsoil or compost.

And finally, once planted don't expect fireworks from the plant straight away; it is putting all its energies into growing a bigger root system below ground.

Perfectly good pruning

Gardens do need 'refereeing' you will need to get in and cut stuff back.

At the beginning of this book I said I would not be delving into the proper technically perfect way to garden, explaining how to prune or how to plant; that information has been written about in every other gardening book and it is not what this book is about. However, gardening does involve picking up forks, spades, secateurs and shears; you will have to cut things, plant things and referee things. But this book is about finding ways to maintain the garden as easily as possible so, horticulturalists may well read with disdain that the advice is not the proper way to do things, but it doesn't matter. I am not aiming for perfection so quick and perfectly good as a method is fine. Let's face it plants have existed for billions of years, survived dinosaurs, meteorites and the ice age so I doubt any 'slightly less than perfect pruning regime' is going cause them real harm!

All plants grow, that just goes with the territory, which results in plants needing to be cut to ensure they don't outgrow the space available, which means you need to know how and when to prune. Thankfully there are some useful rules of thumb that apply and are easy to remember.

- Do the 3D's first; Dead, Diseased or Damaged. Remove all these bits before you think about pruning.
- Try to create an open natural looking shape, so remove more of the stems in the middle and only remove outer stems if they are in the way.

Improving the garden

- If a shrub flowers before May don't cut it back in the autumn. Prune it after it has finished flowering.
- Most shrubs that flower in the summer are best pruned in the autumn or early spring before they start re-growing.
- If a shrub has got tall and leggy AND you can see new leaves appearing on older stems near the bottom of the plant, it will regrow from old wood. Which means you cut the tall leggy growth out; new shoots will emerge from lower down.
- If a shrub or plant only has green growth at the tips of the stems, you can't cut this back hard all over, trim the sides lightly and take a bit more off the top.
- If you aren't sure use the one thirds rule: Remove one third of the branches entirely, one third cut by a half and one third leave well alone. It's a gentler way to prune.
- Don't decapitate the plant with a hedge trimmer, it will just look ugly and won't regrow in the right shape.

Oops!

If you have made a mistake, don't worry most plants will regrow, albeit initially in a rather odd shape. Best then to use the rule of thirds over three years. The plant will be able to grow back into a more natural looking plant again.

What to do with misbehaving plants

Most gardeners aim to create a garden that looks after itself for much of the year, but one that also behaves itself; sadly, this doesn't always happen. We may have inherited a garden with problems or created our own by having the wrong plants.

This section then deals with what to do if …

Plants that get too big

Shrubs will always grow bigger, whether that's taller or wider or both, so at some point we will have to intervene and cut them back. However, how you cut them is important too, do it wrong and you can inadvertently create an ugly looking plant or a garden dome (see Power tools can't prune).

Tip Grower.

Most of these larger plants will be shrubs of some description and these grow in two types of ways:

* *Tip Growers; new growth appears at the end of the branches or stems.*
* *Stem Growers; new growth appears on older stems and at the base of the plant.*

Both need cutting back in different ways to make sure they regrow the way you want them to. Stem growers regrow from anywhere so these can be cut to almost ground level and they will grow back (given a bit of care); tip growers will not tolerate hard pruning and

Stem Grower.

won't regrow from old wood. Tip Growers need gentle trimming every year to keep their shape and size, so if they are too big for the space, there is little option but to remove the plant entirely, you will not be able to make it smaller and it still look nice. Reducing the size of a plant can be done in three ways:

* You can cut it right back for it to regrow (stem growers only).
* You can thin it out, so more light gets in then it doesn't feel so big and imposing.
* Or you can lift the crown which means removing the lower stems or branches letting more light in underneath and allowing other plants to grow.

Rules to Remember:

* If it grows from the tip, trim after it has flowered.
* If it grows from the stem use the One Third's rule to reduce the size.
* Cutting a plant stimulates growth, it will send up lots of new shoots.
* Prune in the spring for plants that flower after May.
* Prune after flowering for plants that flower before May.

Borders that never look good

All plants need three elements to grow well – sunlight, food and water; however, all plants need these three elements in different quantities. No plant will grow well if the balance is not right for them. The upshot is this, if a plant is not growing well where it is situated, it is NOT ever going to grow and look better unless you get the balance right.

Plants won't grow well if they don't get what they need; no matter how much you want them too.

You have two options, first to change the balance where the plant is growing or to change where the plant grows. If you cannot improve light levels or access to food and water then the only option is to move the plant, it will never look good unless you do. The best time to move struggling plants is in the autumn or in the spring.

Flopping plants

Plants always grow toward the light, which is great if the light source (the sun) is above them, but if plants grow in shade or next to fences or walls, the light source is one-sided making the plants grow sideways, grow thinner stems and be more likely to flop.

To reduce the floppiness of the plants in your garden

* Remove overhanging branches to let more sunlight through.

* Make the borders wider so plants aren't tucked 'underneath' the wall when planting.

The stems aren't strong enough to support the flowers.

* Give the plants in the border a bit more space which stops any long thin (weak) stems from growing quickly towards the light; they will grow sturdier instead.

There is another reason plants flop however, and that is to do with breeding. Many modern flower cultivars now have been created to produce more and larger flower heads; big showy flowers sell plants. The downside is that the stems simply can't support the weight of the plant. After every rainfall your prize specimens throw themselves on the floor, which is annoying, and your display looks very despondent. There are solutions though, the obvious being not to buy plants with large heavy flower heads in the first place unless you have also purchased plant supports for them. The second method is known as the Chelsea Chop, each year when the Chelsea Flower Show comes on the TV, pop outside into the garden and cut in half those plants that love to face-plant in the wind or rain.

This may seem a bit drastic, but by shortening the stems, the plant is less likely to flop over once it is in flower. The plant will flower a few weeks later as a result, but that doesn't matter. Chelsea Chopping is hard to do because in May (when this happens) all the plants are looking really lovely and it seems such a shame to cut them; but if you can remember to chop hopefully your garden will not flop!

Unwanted plants

Any plant caught growing somewhere you don't want it to is either a weed or an escapee from another part of the garden. The most fundamental rule with any unwanted plants is to do something about it sooner rather than later, and never let them set seed.

Weeding by hand is better than reaching for the chemical spray

Bare soil will sprout weeds, it always does, weeding is easiest and quickest if the weeds are still seedlings, don't wait to see what they grow into, because many weeds are able to sprout, grow, flower and seed in the blink of an eye!

The perennial weeds are trickier, they have longer deeper roots or they spread via an underground network of roots. There is no alternative but to get down on hands and knees and dig these out as far as possible.

Never use a rotavator or you chop these long roots into thousands of little roots and each piece can produce a new plant. Neither would I advocate applying copious volumes of weed killer, it is a quick fix way of ensuring a longer problem.

Honesty is lovely, but will appear everywhere!

Plants that want to take over the garden

Some plants are speed-spreaders but there are nice speed-spreaders and not so nice spreaders, but the choice as to which type you have is subjective; one person's naturalising is another person's weed! Assuming however, you are not entirely happy the plant is spreading itself all over the garden, here's how do you deal with it.

Firstly, determine how is it spreading, by seed or is it popping up from underground. If the plant spreads by seed, then it is simple to prevent too many seedlings popping up, all you do is remove the spent flowerhead before the seeds ripen.

Alliums do spread everywhere, but that is a good thing!

If, however the plant spreads itself via underground roots or by producing little bulbous off-shoots underground, then the only solution is digging. Remove all the plants, bulbs, and roots from where they are becoming a problem. You will have to keep doing this ad infinitum as the plant doesn't know it is misbehaving, it is just doing its thing and happily growing.

If you do like the plant and want to keep it where it is, then the best containment method is to plant it in a sturdy pot and bury that in the soil.

Weed infested borders

Weeding is the most soul-destroying part of gardening; it is the gardening equivalent of cleaning the toilet. As soon as you are finished, more weed seedlings have popped back up and you must start again! There are two types of weeds, those that set loads of seed each year and those that lurk underground and reappear in perpetuity and your garden will have a mixture of both. Regular weeding (just like toilet cleaning) does keep everything sorted, but even this can sometimes not keep on top of a problem.

If the border is just a mangle of weeds growing in amongst the plants, then the best and most effective long-term solution is to dig all the border plants out and tackle the whole border.

This is best done after a good dollop of rain, ideally in spring or autumn when the soil is softer. Gently lift all the plants you can and plonk them in a bucket of water or a large plastic bag and place the plants in the shade. Then you can get digging over the border removing all the underground roots you can see. Before putting the plants back in, remove any unwanted roots from the root-balls of the plants as well, this can either be done by gently easing them out or wash the soil off completely and then remove the weed roots. The border is then replanted and given a bit of care with regular watering.

This will remove most of the perennial weeds and many of the annual weeds, but there will still be weed seeds that will germinate, there will be fewer of these and as long as they are removed before they flower, you should be able to keep on top of the border more easily in the future.

Plant munching bugs

I have never been an advocate of the wholesale spraying of plants simply because I do not believe killing one pest solves the problem.

Our gardens do not exist in a bubble, they are connected to the wider world, so to try to create a chemical fortress in the garden that protects the plants from all unwanted visitors is impossible. Everything needs to eat something to survive, but if the garden you have is constantly covered in bugs that destroy your plants, the problem the garden has is balance not bugs. Killing the plant munching bugs will not solve the problem.

Nature is a far better at looking after the environment than we are, in fact it is our attempt at 'nurturing the environment' that creates the problems of too many plant munching bugs!

This is not a disaster; it's nature.

There are two long term solutions to this problem, the first and most important is to relax.

It does not matter if there are aphids eating the plants, no-one is going to call the garden police and arrest you for failure to manage the plants properly, the plants will usually grow back.

The second solution is to think long term, this is about how you can reduce the amount of garden maintenance you need to do; the key is to let nature do the pest control for you. This approach takes a little while to get going but in the long term saves you time, money and effort, so it is worth it.

Improving the garden

- Plant more insect friendly flowers.
- Plant more natural looking flowers.
- Avoid using new plant varieties unless you have seen bees or butterflies landing on them.
- Do not spray with anything other than a garlic spray.
- Have a hedgehog hole in the fence.
- Put up insect hotels and some bird boxes.
- Never prune shrubs/hedges/trees in nesting season.

Bees love alliums ...

Nasturtiums: a favourite plant food for bugs and humans alike.

Over a couple of years, the garden will find a level, the bad bugs get eaten by the good bugs; it will not mean there are no plant munching bugs; it's just the garden won't be overridden with them.

Lastly a good technique is to use sacrificial plants; plants no bug can resist. They will happily chomp away at those leaving your prize specimens alone. One of the easiest and best sacrificial plants is the Nasturtium.

Plants don't need to be perfect to look or smell beautiful, in fact plants are quite used to getting eaten in the wider world and they all seem to grow back happily. All we need to do is copy what nature does so well.

Lousy looking lawns

Why do most lawns never look like those on the adverts or in magazines? Well the simple answer is that perfect lawns don't really exist. Having an immaculate weed and ants nest free, flat verdant carpet of green in the back garden is simply an unrealistic goal. As such comparing the patch of

Lawns don't need to be perfect, constantly striving for perfection means you never enjoy what you have

lawn you have with the images portrayed in magazines and adverts does you a disservice, don't compare the lawn to one that an advertiser has dreamt up! So perhaps now, the lawn in the garden is not quite so lousy after all. If it is obvious the grass is struggling to grow, and it looks awful then in general there are three problems that need addressing.

Compaction: We walk on a lawn, so the soil underneath gets flattened and squashed. In the end the soil is so dense the roots can't push through to help the grass grow. The grass then is more easily worn away by the foot traffic.

Just because gardening books show how to get rid of mushrooms in the lawn; it doesn't mean you have to!

Drainage: Usually in conjunction with compaction, water cannot drain away easily, so the roots sit in a cold wet puddle in winter, resulting in the grass dying.

Light: The grass is trying to grow in an area where there is not enough light and it becomes threadbare and scraggy with plenty of bare patches.

Most lawns will grow much better with a spiking, in spring and in the autumn, spike the lawn using a garden fork to lift the soil a little which helps both the reduce the compaction and drainage problems.

If the lawn simply won't grow well in an area because of poor light levels, then you need to stop trying. There are plenty of plants that will form a green carpet in shade to use instead. If those grow happily away, they will invariably look better, grow better and require less effort from you; Moss, Ferns, Ajuga or Galium Oderatum are all good for shady spots.

How to change the garden

Change the garden; just three words but those words mean a lot, they mean you need to change YOUR garden, but do so in such a way that:

* You can enjoy relaxing and sitting in it.

* Can enjoy watching the plants grow the way you want them too.

* Don't spend time on garden chores you hate when you'd rather be doing something else.

* And ensure that once the garden is finished, it will behave itself!

OK, so now maybe it seems a little more daunting, especially if you know very little about plants. The result is that many aspiring gardeners end up marking a lawn in the middle of the garden, digging out a couple of borders, filling them with plants and hoping for the best.

Creating a good garden design is not difficult once you know what you are trying to achieve, it is all a matter of breaking down those three big words into smaller more manageable segments and finding a solution for each segment.

All back gardens have the same fundamental requirements; they need:

* A place to sit and enjoy being outside.

* A way to get to the place you sit all year.

* Somewhere to store all the stuff that goes with having a garden.

Depending on the size of the garden and personal preferences, the relative importance of these elements will differ. For example, in a very small garden the issue of storage is trickier to solve, the garden stuff that needs storing does not shrink in size just because the garden is smaller; but the relative space it uses in the garden, does increase.

Maximising space in any garden is important, but a common error is to assume space can be maximised by making the lawn as large as possible, in fact the reverse is true. The lawn itself becomes the boundary of the usable garden and because the lawn is smaller than the boundary edges, you reduce the usable size of the garden; which makes a small garden feel smaller.

The mathematical principle of 'pareto' also comes into play with garden design. This is the idea that 20% of the garden is used 80% of the time, the other 80% is only used 20% of the time. Consequently, the most important part of the garden to get right is the 20% you use all the time.

So how is the process of changing the garden started?

Rules to remember before you do anything!

Most of this book has so far concentrated on reducing the negative elements of the garden, but if having done that, the garden is still not right you have reached the point where some more structural changes are probably required. As these types of changes tend to be more permanent and expensive, planning is essential as are knowing a few 'tricks of the trade'.

The idea behind this book is to not provide you with a book full of stunning 'ball-gown' type gardens, using our wardrobe analogy again; simply because these images won't help you create or remodel your garden. More important is understanding the theory; if you know why a format works and why it won't; you can apply those theories in your own design. So, let's crack on!

For any garden to feel right and look good it must have met the structural, environmental and emotional elements, but the most important rule to remember, is that the garden must meet your needs and no one else's. However, there are some basic architectural rules that will structurally help the garden look more balanced and better designed.

- ❋ Follow the regulatory line; it connects the house to the garden better.

- ❋ Vertical height should be one third the length of the horizontal space.

- ❋ Closer to the house, there should be more symmetry.

- ❋ Design from the house outward into the garden.

- ❋ Paths need to be at least 76cms (2'6") wide for a person to comfortably walk down, without getting entangled by the plants.

- ❋ Steps: The mathematical formula for getting a 'comfy' step is 2 x height + width = 65cm (or 26 inches for those of you who think imperially).

- ❋ There is a golden ratio which is 1.6: 1; it makes the any rectangle shape look 'right' and not too fat or too skinny.

So, what does this all mean?

What is the regulatory line?

This is all about creating a style to suit the shape of the house. Different types of clothes suit different shapes of people, the same principle applies to houses.

How to change the garden

If the shape of the building is tall and narrow, the garden needs to be more vertical and use taller planting to fill the space from the top to the bottom. If, however, it is a broad wide view, like a bungalow for example, then the design needs to have wider borders to avoid looking 'bitty'. The border design works with the shape of the house linking the two together, the effect being the whole space, house and garden looking like they were made for each other.

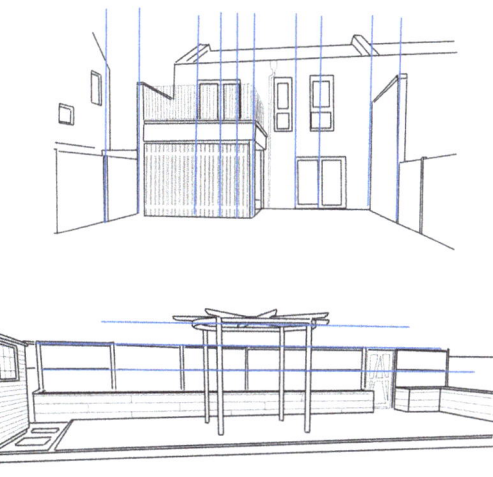

The border needs to 'fit' the shape of the house and garden

The one third's rule

The simplest way to explain this is with a picture. Basically, you need a bit of height in a border, too much and it starts to close in, too little and the border has little impact, you end up staring at fences.

If the height of most of the plants is roughly one third the length of the garden, the whole garden appears more balanced and coordinated. I suppose this could also be called the Goldilocks rule, in that one third is just about right!

Start with more symmetry near the house

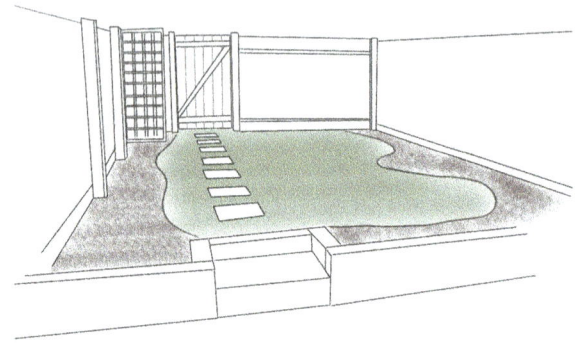

This symmetry is not about creating a symmetrical garden, it about creating a symmetry with the landscape the garden sits in. Mother nature does not 'do' straight geometric design in the world around us, but domestic gardens are not in the wider landscape. Trying to apply natural lines in a small urban garden is like fitting a square peg in a round hole. Urban garden landscapes are dominated by straight lines and strong geometric shapes, especially near the house, it just looks all wrong if you try to force a natural looking shape right next to the walls.

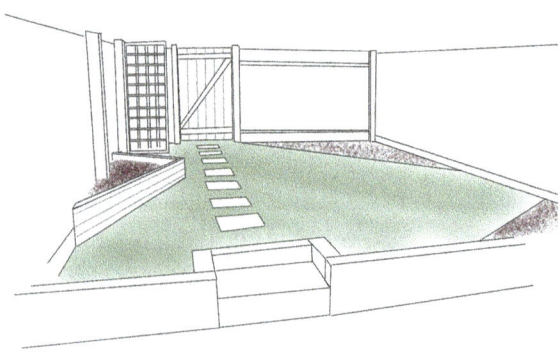

As it is difficult to escape the surrounding geometry, the shapes created in the garden need to be more regular, use arcs, corners, curves, rectangles, squares and circles but not irregular 'amoeba' looking shapes.

Entry into the garden is usually from the back door, so start designing from the house outwards, ask some questions about how you use the garden.

* Where would I normally walk to, a seat, the washing line, the bins?

* How do I get to my most used spots; do I need a pathway?

How to change the garden   55

* Where is the best place in the garden to sit for a morning coffee or to catch the evening sun? Can I sit there in comfort?

* Is there anything that stops me from using the garden how I would like to?

* If so, can I alter it, or do I need to design around it?

These basic questions provide you with a framework to start your design. For example, if the best place to sit is at the end of the garden facing the house, you need a path to get there that is usable all year. Once there, you will want to look at something nice, so this helps you locate the spot for the main border.

The golden ratio

A common garden error is to create borders that are just too narrow; plants hug the fences having been placed side by side tucked into a narrow gap. The unintended result simply highlights the boundaries and fences because the planting line mirrors the line of the fence. The shape of the border has been determined by the garden boundary and is hemmed in by the lawn; resulting in a border squeezed on both sides and a plant display that is rather lacklustre.

Plants always look better in groups rather than planting them side by side along the fence.

The key is to not think about using plants to hide the fence, instead think about creating something interesting to look at that draws your attention away from the fence. The idea is that it is visually better to look at a block of planting rather than a line of planting and the best shape for the block is on a 1: 1.6 ratio.

Rank your garden desires

Every garden is different, as is every gardener, consequently there is no right or wrong garden style, design or planting scheme. The design is only wrong if it does not meet your needs.

To design the garden then, you need to think about what you want it to do and how you want to feel in the garden. Maybe creating a part of the garden that is not overlooked by anyone is important, maybe you need space for the children's toys or that you want to be distracted from the noisy traffic. Obviously, I can't say what's important to you, but if you rank those factors by importance, the changes required begin to reveal themselves, you will know what the garden should be doing for you.

Avoid creating unnecessary work

This is very much 'what is good for the goose is not necessarily good for the gander'. It is going to be your garden, but more importantly you are going to be the one maintaining it. Identifying those chores you dislike, as well as knowing how little time (or energy) you will have for the garden are crucial if you want a garden you can enjoy. If there is only one hour a week for everything in the garden, then lawns, climbing plants, vegetables, bedding plants and hanging baskets are all going to cause you more work than time will allow.

Meadows although pretty aren't terribly tidy gardens.

Similarly, if you absolutely loathe weeding and messy untidy gardens, planting ornamental grasses or a wildflower meadow will not be the right garden for you; no matter how pretty it looks in the pictures.

Designing around problems you can't change

Designing anything would be a whole lot easier if there weren't the immovable obstacles to contend with, and every garden has them. These range from the manhole covers in the wrong place to awkward shaped spaces, over-sized ugly sheds, to the neighbours awful looking fence. There are always parts of any garden you must live with because they can't be changed.

So how can any design work, when the space you have lobs a large sized spanner in the works preventing you from doing what you want? There are three ways of tackling these problems; hide the offending object, beautify that object or create a distraction so it is less noticeable.

Trying to hide a manhole cover by placing a pot on it creates a bigger problem. Now there is a manhole cover and a large pot and both look out of place.

Hiding the Eyesore works if two criteria are met, what you are hiding it with is not in itself going to turn into an eyesore AND the act of hiding it does not create an anomaly in the garden. It does not create a 'why have you put that there' question. The above example of a pot on the manhole cover does just this, you notice the pot and ask why it is there, which is to hide the manhole cover. The result is the eyesore is moved front and centre and is not hidden in any way.

Make an ugly object more attractive by tackling what makes it unattractive

Similarly cloaking an ugly shed in a plant that will grow into a large unruly plant does not hide the shed it simply creates another problem.

Making it look more attractive is another option however, before the said eyesore is repainted, altered or beautified in any way, why it is unattractive needs to be understood because this affects how you need to change it. Ugly boundary fences are a common problem, like this one. It is long, not very attractive and takes up a lot of the view in the garden, now a climber could be grown along the fence, but it will have to be a pretty large climber which means it will be big and heavy and will most likely break the fence.

The fence is an eyesore because it is so visually dominant, there is a lot of it to look at. So, it is not necessarily the panels that are the problem, it's just that there are so many of them. Painting the fence will only convert the red panels to a different colour, which will make it more pleasant to look at, but it won't solve the size problem. The solution is to section the fence into smaller visual chunks, which helps it fade into the background.

Similarly, with ugly sheds (which is a common garden problem), the trick is to transform the shed rather than hide it.

Create a distraction if what is causing the problem can't be made more attractive or cannot be hidden, then distraction is the method to use. The idea is to create something far more attractive and interesting, so your attention is grabbed by that, rather than the eyesore. The best distractions don't just look visually attractive they have to work harder than that. As far as possible all the senses need engaging; sight, sound, touch, smell and taste because that way the brain concentrates processing all those sensory signals it receives at once, which means the solitary eyesore doesn't get noticed as much.

I recently had a client who had a problem with a large shed and wanted to create a border that disguised it, the problem though was that this shed was 100 feet long and 40 feet high! It is not possible to cloak or beautify this kind of structure, so the distraction was to hide the shed in plain sight. The new border needed to run alongside the shed, so we needed to use all our other senses to create a distraction from the size of the shed wall. In this case all the plants attracted pollinators, close inspection of the plants would reveal a whole ecosystem of bees, butterflies, moths and other insects feeding from the flowers all year round. There were scented plants as well as plants that swayed in the wind, all of which drew you in to inspect them; and because the wall was so big, up close it simply becomes a backdrop rather than the large ugly cowshed in the background.

It is possible to make a silk purse out of a sow's ear, you just need to be creative.

There are always solutions to every problem, the trick is to think creatively. Only look to hide an object if the act of hiding it does not itself create an anomaly in the garden. Ugly objects can be made less of an eyesore by tackling the cause of the problem; large objects need visually breaking up, dark corners need lightening and ugly objects can be made more beautiful. If all that doesn't solve the problem, then create a 'look at me instead' part of the garden. It should move and be highly scented, have colours and plants that capture your attention, you can use sculpture or mirrors and lights to create a display that demands to be noticed, all the time.

Tips to improve the garden

It's quite difficult to cater for everyone's design ideals in a single book as we all have unique tastes or ideas, as well as unique gardening environments, but there are some fundamental rules that will guide everyone in the right direction.

- Work with your garden environment; happy plants perform better.

- It is your garden; it does not have to look like the neighbouring gardens.

- Decide what your garden NEEDS to do for you.

- Don't look at glossy garden images for inspiration; these gardens are far too complex and difficult to maintain.

- Write down which parts of gardening you don't like doing.

- Make a list of the things you'd like the garden to have.

- Be realistic; don't overestimate the time you are willing devote to the garden.

- Choose plants by what they WILL DO and not what they look like.

- Be patient; gardens are like a good wine; they improve with age.

"To plant a garden is to believe in tomorrow"
Audrey Hepburn

First time gardeners

The Great Garden Pool of Knowledge

Don't dive right in, just dip your toes in first.

Throughout our lives we pass milestones, some big and some small, some are memorable along with others we'd rather forget. Getting your first ever garden is certainly one of life's more memorable moments. For many that space is often small and is more likely be a courtyard or a small garden; but it is your space to create, enjoy, look after, and make your own.

The key piece of advice to take on board at this stage though, is not to get too ambitious too quickly. Plants have a nasty habit of growing, Nature doesn't stop just because you haven't had time to get in the garden, consequently it is always better to start slowly.

Do's and don'ts for garden newbies:

The premise for this book being written is to show how you can create and maintain a garden that works for you, at a time when your garden experience is negligible; this is a starter book, so with that in mind; this is my advice for all you first timers out there:

Think hard about your time; it is all too easy to create unnecessary work in the garden. If you over-estimate the amount of time you really have available to garden, the garden will quickly run away with you.

Don't try to do too much too soon.

Start with a few simple ideas; for example, if you want food to eat, start with herbs first, progress to easy, high yield veg like tomatoes. Choose plants that thrive on neglect, in case you forget to deadhead or water, like grasses and bulbs.

Buy second hand or at car boot sales; garden tools, equipment and garden pots are expensive, buying preloved items gets you started without having spent too much money first.

Power tools; think carefully whether you really need them. Over-pruning is far easier with a power tool, in addition storage is always an issue in a small garden.

Plants; buy smaller plants, these are cheaper than show stopping specimens. Sweet talk family, friends and neighbours into donating plants from their gardens too. Beware of what you are planting, ask first why they may be happy to part with a plant (see plants that misbehave).

Patience; don't rush, creating a garden is a process and always has been. Instant fix speedy makeovers often result in poorly thought through ideas.

Talk to gardeners; ask any of your friends or family where they have gone wrong, what would they have changed or wished they hadn't planted. It's the 5P's, proper preparation preventing poor performance.

Starting the design process

So, what should you as a garden first timer think about, how should you begin creating or changing the first piece of the outside you have ever owned? More often than not, gardening newbies dive into the great garden pool of data to find tips, hints and ideas to take home. The problem is though what to do with all those tips, hints, pictures and ideas once you plonk them in your garden; thankfully there is a way.

The key piece of advice is KNOW YOURSELF, creating a garden you like and enjoy being in depends on one thing: the garden must 'float your boat' and no one else's. It doesn't matter whether the garden mirrors a design style or has or hasn't got a lawn for example; what matters is that you like using it.

All this means that you need to begin to make a list of what you like and what you don't like. You do not need to choose a design style, at this early stage. The problem of choosing a style category first, is that you end up creating the garden to suit the style rather than creating the garden to suit you.

Garden stuff I enjoy

Deadheading flowers
Sitting under the tree
Sunbathing
Tidying the garden

Once you have a broad list of requirements, you need to prioritise, which parts can be included in your first garden and which can't. It will be impossible to cater for everything, so choose the most important factors for you and work a plan around those.

For example, it may be that you never want to eat outside, but you love sunbathing, in which case sun lounger space supersedes the bistro table and chairs.

Then you need to consider the actual space you have and what you can achieve. Most first-time garden spaces tend to be one of two types, an outside paved area such as a courtyard or a proper garden complete with grass and a few plants. Common to both is the likelihood that it will probably be urban, usually small and is most likely overlooked by the neighbours.

So how do you start and what questions should be asked?

Courtyard Spaces

Beware: Sun traps, difficulty watering plants, storage issues, permanently shaded areas, plant debris and most importantly maintaining usability.

The best way to create a garden in a small space is to think backwards, by which I mean to create the design around what you absolutely need to

have. Once you know how much space is taken up by what you need, you'll know how much space will be left available for decorative bits like plants. The garden's space needs to be split up into virtual blocks which are then 'fitted together' as efficiently as possible to make the best use of the limited area. Plan in order of priority so; seating, then walking, then storage, then planting, as this helps minimise the amount of dead space in the garden.

All any small garden really needs is a place to sit out, however seating areas use more space than you may think. People use the same amount of seating space (i.e. you and your chair) whatever size garden you occupy, the problem is all the space immediately around and above the seating area becomes dead space, you can't put anything there. The design should then block out the table and chairs area, then mark on where you would walk or move around the garden normally and block this area out too and so on.

Creating your first ever garden is an exciting time, but it is all too easy to get carried away. If aspiration exceeds ability, the garden can quickly become overwhelming, leaving you feeling disappointed. Gardening is a skill that is acquired over time, it is far better to start small and build up; be successful before becoming more ambitious.

The courtyard now has a place to sit both near the house and at the end of the garden. Taller planting provides some shade, as well as privacy and all the planters are moveable meaning the design is also versatile.

Plants are jolly expensive and have a nasty habit of dying, especially in the hands of new gardeners; so to begin with, choose plants that are tolerant of neglect and are cheap to replace, just in case!

Useful design tips:

* Have as large a table as you can fit in (extendable preferably), balancing a dinner plate on your knee is no fun.

* Put the seating area in the nicest (sunniest) part of the courtyard and then plan around that space.

* Work out where you walk in the courtyard and keep those lanes free from plants, pots or anything overhead.

* Don't have hanging baskets, they create too much dead space around them.

* Movability; everything must be easy to move, so put any pots on wheels.

* If privacy is an issue, use parasols or screens instead of plants, you only really need privacy if you are sitting outside, using plants as a screen could shade the garden and reduce light levels too much.

* Use mirrors and garden art to add extra interest, it will take up less space and be easier to look after.

* Buy smaller and more commonly available plants, just in case you haven't mastered the art of gardening and the plants don't survive, it won't have cost too much money.

* Evergreen plants and bulbs are good, there is less mess and they are better at looking after themselves.

It's your first garden with real plants

Beware: Inherited mistakes, over ambition, well intentioned advice and blindly copying gardening convention.

This is it then, you have a garden with plants maybe a lawn and a responsibility to keep them alive, the pressure is on to prove you can do this and not let your garden become the one the neighbours sigh and tut about in a disapproving fashion.

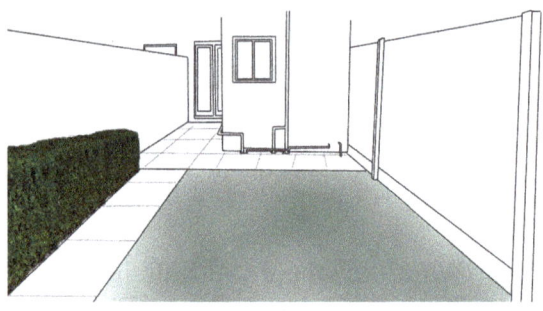

OK, you've got the garden, so now what?

To begin with the three most important garden tools you need are a pen, a notebook and a camera.

Don't get too ambitious to start with, remodel the garden with what's there first and only add a few new plants.

It is highly likely you have inherited a garden from either the previous owners or you have a green square of garden that has been provided by the housing developer, either way right now it's not yet your garden and you don't know how it behaves. You need to find out how you will use the garden and find out which parts of the current layout work with you and which don't.

You need to know, where you drag the chair to sit outside. When you don't use the garden and why? Is there a lack of privacy, is the garden is too windy for you to enjoy? Taking photos on sunny days or rainy days, in the summer and in the winter, all help when planning how to change the garden.

You need to know how it behaves on a good day and how it misbehaves on a bad one.

Over time the rule of 80:20 will likely emerge, in that you use 20% of the garden space 80% of the time. This is the 20% you need think about the most.

Write down what caused you a problem over the year; this could be anything from overhanging branches, light sucking hedges, plants that grew in all the wrong places or that constantly needed attention.

20% of the garden gets used 80% of the time; so, get that 20% right

Creating a garden, you can use and really enjoy is sometimes not about changing everything to something new, sometimes it is just about putting right the things that are wrong. Re-modelling and moving plants around is much cheaper and usually far easier than creating something new.

This is your first ever garden and you are going to make mistakes, it is better to make those initial mistakes with the plants you inherited and haven't had to pay for.

Drawing the design

You may have noticed that so far in this book I have hardly mentioned design planting styles and there is a good reason for this. If you start by deciding on a style for the garden, you tend to fit your checklists to that style rather than creating a garden with all the elements you need. The better method is to get the design shapes for the space right first, then adapt the style by using different materials, textures and colours to create the finished look.

For example, if you preferred a more natural look, then the raised borders in the design could be made using reclaimed bricks or logs, whereas if you preferred a more modern look you might use new wooden sleepers.

The basic shape is the key part to get right, we are back to our wardrobe analogy again; if the underwear fits well, whatever outfit is chosen to be worn will look good because underneath everything is being held in the right place.

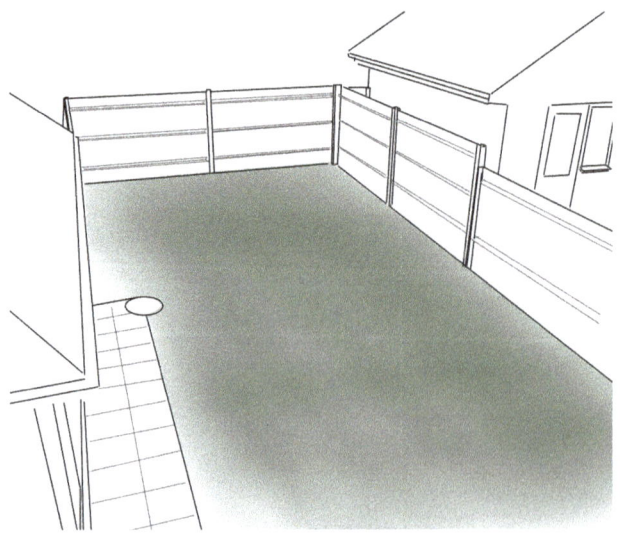

Brand new gardens with nothing in them can be daunting; having a blank canvas is tricky!

Start with the big shapes first

The shapes to deal with first are the lawn, the seating area, the path, and if you have one, the shed, because these are the elements that in a small garden are going to take up most of the view in the garden. You need to take some time playing around with different layout options until the right design pops out; and it will, you will at some point think: 'well, that would work'. Which is all a design process is; working out what will look most right in your garden.

The Lawn

In any small garden the lawn area will normally take up most space and the shape of the lawn will be by far the most noticeable element in the garden. Keep to a simple lawn shape, a square, oval, circle or rectangle. These will be easier to maintain, mark out and mow.

Play around with the shapes first until they look right, which incidentally these don't.

However, they don't need to be 'whole' shapes. If part of the square is cut out, the lawn will still be a square shape in your mind's eye, it will still look right.

This is handy because it now means that shape can rotate, be offset or partly hidden to make the garden look more interesting. Do not create a weird shaped wobbly blob of a lawn; that will never look right. Lawns, are not an essential part of a garden and don't need to be included in the design, only include a lawn if you know having one will be beneficial.

The Seating

The only point of a purpose-built seating area is to enable you to sit in the garden on a flat, level surface that will not get eroded or worn out by the action of feet, or the scraping of chairs and tables. It provides an all-weather surface enabling you to use the garden for most of the year. This seating area can be any hardwearing surface, the only design requirements are that it is in the part of the garden you prefer to sit and that it is large enough to sit at comfortably. This main seating area can also be part of the lawn, although the grass may become overly worn.

The Path

Paths take us places in the garden, they are not simply a walkway to the end of the garden. For a path to 'work' it must be usable for most of the year, easy to walk down and it must take a logical route. Simply creating a meandering windy path down a garden will not ensure the path is used. If it goes the wrong way, people will shortcut around it and create their own paths. A path

This path is usable, easy to walk down and takes a logical route, but maybe let's itself down with the 'concrete runway' look!

will also dissect a garden, which can make the garden look bitty and narrow. Once again, a path is not necessary if there is nowhere to go in the garden. Only include a path if you need one.

In any small garden, paths are visually dominant, your eye will automatically follow the path to its end, so if both path and its destination are unsightly, the whole garden will be affected.

The Shed / Storage Space

Anyone who has a garden will have garden stuff and that stuff needs to be stored when not in use. Ideally it can all get stowed away in a garage, but if that is not possible, then storage is needed. Normal garden convention would recommend the shed is popped at the end of the garden, but is this really the best place for it to go? The reason sheds tend to be plonked as far from the house as possible is that they are not attractive features, the hope is by building it at the end of the garden the shed will become invisible, but that sadly doesn't work.

Sheds become unintended garden features simply because a path is built to get to the shed. The path then leads the eye straight to the ugliest part of the garden. The shed must function as a storage space but just because it has a boring function, it does not mean the shed has to be boring or hidden away. Instead of thinking how you can hide the storage away somewhere, think the reverse, how can the shed be made part of the garden, what is the best way to hide this in plain sight; how can the shed be made beautiful.

Combining the Shapes

How you 'set' the lawn into the garden can have some additional designing benefits too, the garden can be made to look wider by simply rotating the shape of the lawn. The easiest way to work out the best layout is to take a picture from an upstairs window, digital technology now allows us to draw directly onto the screens, making playing around with different ideas easy. The shape of the lawn will then create leftover spaces, these are where the plants and the storage areas will go. It doesn't matter that these leftover shapes are odd shapes or sizes, the planting will easily disguise this.

But what of the shed you may ask, the shed will most likely be an 8' x 6' rectangle, that won't fit in these odd shaped

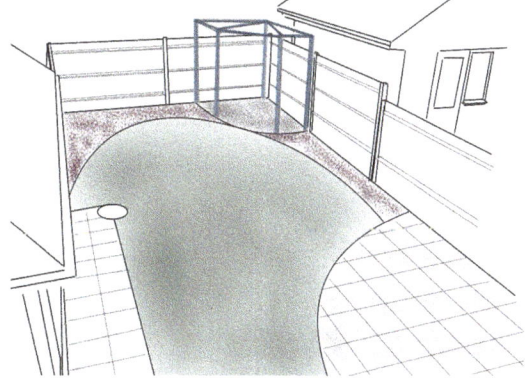

The curves of the patio and lawn work together.

leftovers. The simple answer is why does the shed have to dictate to the garden, why can't the garden dictate the shape of the shed? Most power tools fold away so sheds no longer need to be shed shaped. Ask then; is a standard shed shape really required or can you unleash your inner designer to create a storage space that fits your garden instead?

Planning the Planting

Sticking to a colour theme is a good idea, you colour match your wardrobe, so do the same in the garden; but perhaps it's best to avoid this combination.

Undoubtedly this is the trickiest aspect, if you aren't sure what a Heuchera is, how on earth would you know whether your garden would benefit from having one! Once again, I find the analogy of a wardrobe of clothes a useful design tool, because we can break down the plant choices into the equivalent items of clothing; it is much easier shopping for a pair of blue jeans, size 10, than shopping for a complete top to toe outfit.

The underwear is already in place, the shape of the borders within the garden design has been created, now you need to work out what the border will wear. Any outfit starts with items of clothing from our wardrobe essentials. These are your jeans, favourite jumpers, etc., that look good all the time, different tops are worn to create new outfits, and these are finished by adding a few accessories. Planning the planting for a border uses the same process; you need a few dependable, reliable 'look good all year' plants in the border and then you can change the look by having different tops to wear with these. The spring top may be yellow and blue, and then a new top is worn for the summer which may be yellow, orange and red for example. The plant equivalent of an accessory is any plant that adds to the display for a short period of time, the accessories I always prefer to use are bulbs.

Just like with your wardrobe, you would never (one hopes) dream of mixing yellow, orange, pink, blue, peach and purple in the same outfit, because unless you are Vivienne Westwood, it is a look that is hard to pull off. Instead we all tend to stick to a base colour and add one or two colours to create an outfit.

As a garden owner, your job in choosing the planting for the border is to ask two questions;

> *How does this plant like to grow?*
> *How do I need the plant to grow?*

Ideally the two answers should be the same, if not then you run the risk you are planting a problem.

Working out what you need to plant is best started by working out what you need the plant to do. Each border created will have its own unique environment and it will have a particular purpose, all that's needed is to make sure the plants used are suitable for both. For example, one border may be near the main seating area, so the 'outfit' here would look good if it was light and flowing, used soft tactile plants with wonderful scents in bright happy colours – so it's more summer outfit rather than a formal tailored suit and tie style. Even if you don't know what plants to put in, you probably now have an image in your mind's eye of how it will start to look. This is a real help when you come to choosing plants, you don't need to know the name, you just need to find a plant that fits the style and mood required. Although most garden centres list the plants by type and then alphabetically, knowing you need a soft textured airy plant with bright happy flowers means you can walk up and down the aisles until you find one that fits the job description.

Planting with 'boxes'

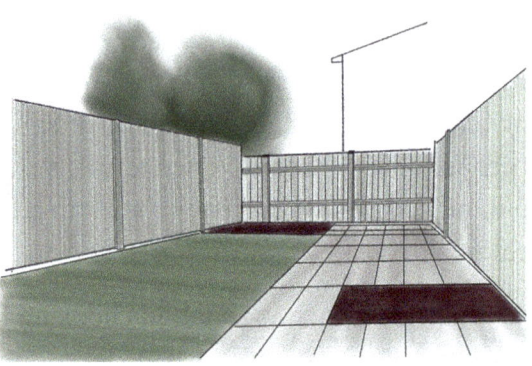

Traditionally garden borders have followed the same design formula, taller plants at the back, shorter at the front, it is a style that works; however, it isn't the only option. It is the only layout available if the borders created are long and thin, the problem being that putting the taller plants at the back by the fence, leads to them flopping over the ones at the front. By using the design methods already described, the border shapes that can now be created by the lawn and seating areas may no longer be thin rectangles that follow the fence lines; which means you are no longer constrained by the 'taller plants to the back' design style.

All plants inhabit a box of space, this is not the shape of the plant, it is the area of space the plant uses up. These boxes come in a variety of shapes and sizes, if we know the size and shape of the box the plant will use up in five years' time, creating the border simply involves putting boxes together to create a well-balanced look.

There are four basic shapes of box;

- Inverted pyramid; trees and some larger shrubs.

- Cubes; in a variety of sizes.

- Rectangles; plants that spread wider than they are tall or low ground huggers.

- Columns; plants such as grasses or taller flowering perennials.

Each box can be a different colour, which allows you to plan the layout easily. Once you have the layout sorted, the wardrobe comes back into play, each box is assigned as an item of clothing (in other words what is it's job specification, why do you need it), now can you see the outfit created and whether that outfit is balanced and not simply made up with only accessories and a couple of pairs of jeans.

The other major advantage in planning a layout with this method is logistical, once you have the boxes in place, knowing how many plants will be needed is simply a matter of counting the boxes. Because each box represents the size in five years' time, the border won't get overfilled or squashed together, it will look fine now but will look even better once everything has grown together. If the border needs a little extra help, accessories can be popped in any gaps to provide complimentary colour at different times of the year.

Tips for deciding what to plant:

* Decide the job the plants need to do first.

* Plan the outfit; what colour tops for which seasons.

* Decide on the style of the outfit, business suit, afternoon tea, or day at the races, etc.

- ❉ Build with coloured boxes to create a balanced look.
- ❉ Only add accessories that complement the outfit.

Planting a border is one of the most enjoyable parts of gardening, hopefully this method will provide a framework that helps making the planning of these borders or the changing of an existing border much easier and less reliant on impulse buying and guesswork.

Outfit 1: A soft and floaty 'summer dress'

Outfit 2: One for the beach perhaps?

Garden styles and why they don't work

Garden design has traditionally classified gardens into a few well-known styles; Mediterranean, Cottage, Modern, Contemporary, Natural, Dry and Tropical, plus a few others. No garden or style of design can ever be perfect though, knowing the pitfalls and problems each type of gardening has, will help prevent costly errors. It's back to those 5P's again, proper planning preventing poor performance.

Mediterranean gardens

This style is all about memories of past summer holidays, spent sitting in warm perfumed gardens surrounded by bright and colourful flowers. It is also a style created (mistakenly) with the view that having a garden of drought loving plants must be lower maintenance, because those plants won't need as much water or feeding.

This style generally uses lots of hard landscaping in white, raised borders, hard edges, stones mulches, bright vibrant colours (no pastel shades). Spiky plants, grey leaves, big pots and a more spartan planting style. It's crisp, bright and clean.

Mediterranean gardens work because of the hot sun and sparse summer rain, plants grow slowly and so do the weeds. Our summers are cooler and wetter, but our winters are cold and damp and it's here the problem lies; Mediterranean plants hate soggy bottoms. Cold wet waterlogged ground will quickly kill off these specimens. In addition, our cooler wetter climate causes algae to grow, turning your pristine white gravel or whitewashed walls a pea-soup green; weed seedlings thrive growing under gravel mulches and in the autumn wet leaves fall down smothering said gravel; consequently maintenance is high if you want to keep these gardens looking neat and clean.

Cottage gardens

These gardens are synonymous with 'chocolate box' images of thatched cottages hemmed in by a bucolic mix of plants all vying for position and flowering their socks off.

Hard landscaping is kept to a minimum apart from a few rustic looking poles holding up a vast canopy of pastel coloured roses. It looks stunning and because it appears to have been created using the 'got a space, pop a plant in' style of gardening, it would appear an easy style to replicate, what could possibly go wrong?

Anything goes in a cottage garden, there are few formal structured shapes, it's more rustic and shabby chic. Pastel colours abound and the planting density is high.

Although our climate is well suited to this cottage garden style, it is quite hard to achieve this natural looking but abundantly flowering idyll. The idea is for the planting to be thick and dense; the plants are supposed to hold each other up or so it seems. The reality though is that usually, lots of plant supports are used along with lots of hidden corsetry. Plants are tied to stakes and other less visible structures to ensure everything behaves. Cottage gardens always look their best in summer, but as many of the plants die down in winter, you may not get enough of a show for the whole year to make this style worthwhile having; especially if your garden is small.

Contemporary or Modern Gardens

This design style treats the garden as an outside room which is equipped with any number of mod-cons. Bespoke seating, lighting displays, outside televisions, fire pits and hot tubs; are deemed desirable garden

assets. The planting tends to be big and showy, usually in muted colour palettes (you are supposed to notice the décor not the plants). Most contemporary gardens are cool, sharp, chic and need to look immaculate or they lose the essence of why they were built. All of which mean the garden will demand attention to keep it looking the way you want it to. Falling leaves look out of place, all the plants need to behave and grow in the desired way or the sharp straight lines and uncluttered look many of these gardens aspire too is easily overgrown.

Clearly contemporary gardens can be stunning and beautiful, but these can also be high maintenance gardens too.

Dry or Tropical Gardens

The aim of any garden like this is to recreate a little bit of somewhere else in the world in the back garden, so for new gardeners or those who aren't keen on gardening; recreating a type of planting from another part of the world will require more expert knowledge and experience if it is to succeed.

It will depend on what is being created, but one will involve a lot of stone and arid planting, the other big leaves and

This is a Strelitzia or bird of paradise plant.

plenty of green. The skill in creating these gardens comes from working out how to adapt the style to our climate and weather, which will mean protecting plants from winter rains, moving plants indoors or adding watering systems to ensure the large leaves get enough water and so forth.

Clearly for all those of you reading this book, it's probably not the best style to adopt if you are after an easy-care garden.

Natural (Eco-friendly) Gardens

Eco-friendly gardens are often portrayed as resembling a hippy/1970's Good Life format, grass is left unmown, an eclectic mix of various bird, bat and insect hotels dangle from every nook and cranny, climbers are left to consume structures and the garden looks untidy and a bit neglected, so I can perfectly understand why many would-be gardeners feel an eco-friendly garden is not a style for them, although having a wildlife friendly garden would be.

There is another natural eco-friendly garden style though that is more urban garden friendly. This halfway house combines the need for a usable garden with a desire for it to be a place for wildlife. To that end, this is how I would envisage a natural eco-friendly garden.

It can be any style, shape, size or design you choose, the important part is this: at least 80% of the plants in the garden provide food for insects, butterflies and bees for at least 80% of the year.

The fundamental relationship you have with the garden also needs to change; the garden is no longer a

Apparently, bees might actually be able to count the spots on the petals; nature's equivalent of painting by numbers.

place to show off your horticultural prowess, instead it becomes more of a place you enjoy interacting with nature. The role of the gardener becomes less about control and transforms to that of a referee. It is fine if some plants have caterpillars chomping the leaves because you understand that controlling the food chain via the use of chemical sprays causes your garden long term damage.

Creating an ecological balance in the garden is more important, because it is this natural balance that will help reduce the volume of unnecessary gardening chores. High end predators are encouraged because they deal with pests far more effectively than chemical sprays, lawns don't have to be weed and moss free, nor cut to under an inch. It's a garden where you have decided that your little plant patch has a role in helping save the planet, and realising gardens that look only good, at the expense of the natural world, are no longer worth the effort.

For the inexperienced gardener it's the easiest garden style to create of all and arguably the best.

Common garden mistakes

Life would be so simple if we got everything right first time, but sadly we don't. Learning to garden, creating a new garden or remodelling an existing one involves making many decisions. Hopefully the vast majority we will get right, but some we won't. The trouble is many of the gardening bloopers created can be extremely expensive and or time consuming to put right so knowing how designs or well-intentioned ideas could go wrong is really useful. Here are some common design errors and planting mistakes so you can avoid making them too!

Centrifuge planting

Centrifuge planting; the act of flinging the borders to the edges of the garden. This style although extremely common, has arisen because of a misconception over how to make the best use of the space in the garden.

Ok, so the borders don't take up too much space, but it hardly stops you in your tracks does it?

Gardeners want to maximise the available space and wrongly assume this is best achieved by having a large open space in the centre of the garden with borders around the boundaries. The plants are evenly spread around the boundaries to 'fill the space better' and hide the fences, but the resulting garden only emphasises the boundaries whilst underwhelming with the display.

Creating fewer but more impressive groups of plants gives depth to the planting, there is more to see than a single line of planting squashed next to a fence. This creates an impression that the garden is larger than it is, it feels bigger even if it's not.

Creating a lawn that sits in the centre of the garden and which is as large as possible is intended to create the feeling of space, nothing gets in your way as you walk round the garden; but it also creates a wide-open space with nothing there too. There is nowhere to hide should you wish to; you have created the effect of a goldfish bowl of a garden, where you swim around the middle and can be seen by everybody. Whilst being overlooked may not bother some people, being in a goldfish bowl garden may result in the garden not being used as much as it should be. Centrifuge planting simply creates an open but largely underused space.

A better approach is to combine all the plants into one or two big borders that don't have to follow the fence lines. The plants have more space to grow, better access to the light and the deeper fuller planting makes a more impressive

display. Placement of the borders can also help create more secluded areas, helping make the garden a more enjoyable, user friendly place to be.

Don't just stand there, do something

Inaction is the main contributing factor that exacerbates any problem. We have all committed the odd planting faux pas whether it's a plant that grows too fast or is one that seeds itself everywhere you don't want it to. However, the key to getting and keeping on top of your garden is to do something about it.

Garden mistakes won't fix themselves.

Plants will only ever get bigger and the problem become worse unless you deal with it at source. Constantly cutting down plants in the vain hope it will somehow learn to fit the space just won't work. If you inadvertently make a mistake, the sooner you sort it out and start again, the better.

Faking nature

Most gardens in urban areas are surrounded by straight lines and geometric shapes consequently attempting to create a natural landscape by adding curvy wobbles to paths and lawn shapes will just look odd. If you do not want to use straight lines, use arcs and curves instead.

Natural looking planting in a formal setting works.

To make the garden look and feel more natural, use open flowers, avoid the more modern varieties and allow the plants to grow into their natural shape. The combination of this style of planting albeit growing in a framework of regular shapes for the lawn and paths and borders, will look far more effective.

Heads, shoulders, knees, and toes

When you walk along the street, do you stare at your feet, do you greet friends by looking down at their knees, of course not, we stare straight ahead. We view the world first at eye-level and then we shift our gaze left, right, up and down, why then are so may flower beds planted with plants that only grow as high as our knees?

The border is a 3-dimensional box so, fill it!

If you are looking to plant a border you need to start by thinking about what will be seen at your eye-level.

Starting from the toes upward creates a problem; all the space in the border at the bottom becomes filled up. The only option left available to hide a fence or boundary is with a climber as this does not take up space at ground level.

The brick wall is what you see, the new border now makes you look at the plants.

This climber grows up the fence and toward the light, thus reducing light levels for the plants below – which don't grow so well, they are effectively trying to grow under a dark umbrella.

The result is top growth hanging down, nothing in the middle and a few paltry looking plants stuffed in at the bottom.

Invisibility cloaks don't work

Garden sheds are not the most attractive feature in any garden but trying to hide them can be a mistake too, simply growing a climber over a shed to hide it ends up creating a second bigger problem; it takes a big robust usually vigorous plant to cloak a shed. Pruning becomes increasingly difficult as the climber takes hold, the ugly shed just gets covered by a large unruly plant making it even more of an eyesore.

Grasses are also great distractors when the wind blows

The best advice is to hide the shed in plain sight. Start by painting the shed, but don't use 'shed brown' or 'not very invisible green' instead choose a colour that compliments or contrasts with the flowers in your garden.

Making the shed more attractive removes its ugly element, but the shed is still very noticeably a shed; it needs a better 'invisibility cloak', this is achieved by making another part of the garden demand your attention more. The garden needs a 'look at me instead' border, which is eye-catching and attention seeking. This border really needs to command attention, it can be created with colour and should use plants that move. Having a border that dances in

How about a log wall for the shed for example?

the breeze or that attracts bees and butterflies will capture your interest much more than the shed will.

Creating a better and more attractive garden sometimes involves not tackling the problem head on.

Paltry Patios

Patios are expensive to build, sadly all too often they are built the wrong size and in the wrong place; risking the emergence of an expensive white elephant. The problem arises because how you need to use the patio is often not properly thought through.

This is not a usable patio.

Patio convention often builds a paved area outside the back door running the width of the house; the patio design is created to fit the house; the problem is the patio does not fit with you.

You won't use a patio just because you have one, you use the patio because it helps you enjoy your garden as you want to. In any small space all the elements need to function well, the patio will become the most used area of the garden, it needs to be sited in the nicest part of the garden.

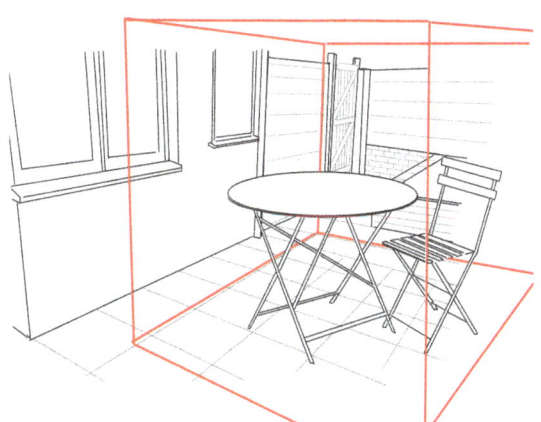

Even a small bistro table and chair will occupy a large box of space if you want to sit outside comfortably.

It is also easy to underestimate how much space humans take up, making the patio too small means you won't use it as much as you should. You need to add both sitting space and access space to the area around where table will be sited. For example a small round table 60cm in diameter takes an area of 0.3 metre square, but when you add chairs and space to sit at the table, the space required expands to 2m in diameter and that's before you have factored in being able to walk round the table too. Patios need to be comfortable, none of us love shoehorning ourselves into a tight corner and feeling squashed up sitting at a table, so give yourselves enough room, if that means having a smaller lawn; so be it.

Unfortunately, if you have inherited a paltry sized patio that you can't use, there is only one real option and that is to create a new one in a better area.

Pathways to hell by Tread Carefully

This is the one part of 'knowing how to garden' I wished I had understood before I ever constructed my first garden. The fateful mistake made was choosing a path material because it looked nice, rather than choosing a path material that was best suited for the environment of the garden. I got my decision-making priorities wrong and was summarily 'punished' by the path for many years, the wrong choice of material created so much unnecessary work.

This path is great, it is functional, interesting, attractive and environmentally friendly.

The golden rule for creating a path that really works is to think about the debris first, what will need clearing up from that path; then ask whether the material to be used, makes that job easier or harder.

This approach ensures you minimize time taken with chores, there are plenty of path materials to choose from but choosing the wrong material turns what should be a quick task into hard labour.

Path rules:

- Under trees: it must be easy to sweep, rake or blow debris away.

- Anywhere in shade, avoid light coloured paving, no decking, or smooth polished paving surfaces. Wet slippery green algae will appear whether you like it or not.

- In a sunny spot avoid dark colours, unless you like burned feet.

- Edging a lawn; never edge lawns with loose stones ... ever!

- Bird droppings; avoid the more porous stone slabs and avoid dark colours.

- Barefoot lovers; don't have any gravel mulches where you like walking.

- Well-used paths must be hardwearing; don't rely on grass.

- Paths near the house; remember shingle gets walked into the house on the soles of shoes.

- Frequently wet; don't use super smooth paving surfaces, use textured pavers or loose stone.

A path is a route from one place to another, it has a purpose. If the path cannot fulfil that role it becomes a waste of space. If you cannot walk on the path in winter because it is too muddy or slippery or you can't walk along the path without getting whacked in the face by an errant tree branch; the path is no good.

Creating an unsuitable path just means wasting valuable space. The path must be functional, but this doesn't have to consign the path to be a just ugly slab of concrete either, function can look gorgeous too.

Deciding the route the path takes, determines the design of the garden

Design rules to think about:

* A comfortable width of a path is the width of a doorway; but think in three dimensions, it is not the width at your feet that is most important; the width of the path at head height is what matters.

* Paths should take the most logical route to where they need to go, or people cut corners.

* A wobbly path does not make you meander slowly through the garden!

* Steppingstones need to be a lady's stride length not man's stride length.

* The path does not have to be the same width along its entire length.

* Paths that run down the middle of a garden tend to make gardens appear narrower.

* Solid straight concrete paths look more like mini runways.

* If the path follows the line of the fence, it will make the fence more obvious.

Things you didn't think paths could do ...

Paths can really help with the design because they are a visually dominant feature in any garden. A good path has a positive effect, conversely a bad path has a negative visual effect. Paths link spaces, paths move your eye along the garden and paths can also deceive the eye into thinking there is more to come.

Play with the garden perspective. Paths that are offset from the line of the fencing can make a garden look wider. If the width of the path varies, parts of the garden can be made to appear further away or closer. If the path has an entrance, it makes you want to walk through. Similarly, if the path goes around a corner (that you can't see around) curiosity makes you want to find out what's there. Just ensure there is something there to see or do, like a statue or a seat for example.

Paths need a destination then they have a purpose. If that destination is just the shed, it's a bit disappointing, have something you arrive at as well as the shed!

What you walk on matters

One of the underlying aims of this book is to change how we all think about our gardens and challenge established gardening conventions. We all need to do our bit in reducing and reusing to help mitigate the negative aspects of human life. It matters what you use to create and subsequently maintain your path. All paving slabs are quarried, transported, manufactured and delivered to garden centres or builder's merchants.

Indian Sandstone for example, is quarried and transported from either China or India; ask the supplier whether it has been ethically sourced. Know that your new patio has not been built at the expense of another natural environment in another part of the world.

Will you have to resort to chemical weed-killers to keep the path clear and do you want to keep spraying poisons onto the ground? Is having a totally weed free path essential and if so, are there other less poisonous solutions available. Is the path or paving area permeable also, where does the rainwater run off too, will this cause a problem?

These may seem small points, but collectively these small changes make a massive difference.

Privacy; it's all about perspective

In the film *Apollo 13* starring Tom Hanks, there is a famous clip of him standing outside at night holding his arm aloft and hiding the moon with just the tip of his thumb. Making your garden more private or feeling more private involves the same principle; perspective.

The worst design mistake that arises from our desire for privacy is that we build walls around our garden. The result is a big green wall surrounding the garden, that uses up garden space and overpowers other plants. Thankfully though this is not the only solution to the privacy problem.

No one can see in, but you can't see out either.

An enclosed garden may make us feel more secure, we all like to know that our home is our castle and so forth, but often these walls become impenetrable barriers that end up cutting us off instead. These green walls eat into the space available and block out the sunshine. As such barriers and walls are blunt instruments in the desire for privacy.

We can be a little smarter, we just need to think like Tom.

If you sit in your favourite part of the garden and look about, where exactly are you overlooked from? Often it will be from upstairs windows, but could strategically placing an object that blocked the view from that window to where you were sitting (i.e. Tom Hanks thumb) make the garden feel more private?

The key point here is that we are not trying to make all the garden private, just making more private the part of the garden we enjoy sitting in the most. One tall strategically placed plant is maybe all that's needed to give you a sense of privacy. Losing the big green wall mentality may be a difficult concept but the advantage of doing so is that the garden will be less of an enclosed box and starts being more a place we can enjoy the wider world.

Concentrate on making private the place you like sitting in the most.

Trellis troubles

Using trellis is a great way to bring plants up to head height, the flowers are right in front of our eyes and so are any wonderful scents.

Sadly, though many planted trellis fail to deliver the spectacular display hoped for; more commonly the trellis is covered by a tangled mess of what looks more like overcooked spaghetti falling off the top of the trellis, or the flowers sit atop this spaghetti where they can't be enjoyed. So, what has gone wrong?

The three main problems that occur with trellis and climbing plants.

* The wrong sort of trellis is used.

* The wrong plant is growing on the trellis.

* The siting of the trellis is wrong.

Which type of trellis is best?

There are two main types of climber; those that are planted in the spring, flower in summer and then die back; these are the Annual climbers. These tend to grow no more than two metres in any season, so plants such as some Clematis or Thunbergia. Then there are the Everlasting climbers, plants like Wisteria, Roses, Honeysuckle and Parthenosissus. These come in a few size categories; large and heavy, really large and really heavy or requires a tree to support it.

I think you can see there's a bit of a theme here already.

Annual climbers

Let's deal with annual climbers, things like Sweet Peas, Nasturtiums, Black Eyed Susan etc. These are short lived, thin stemmed, lightweight and not very thuggish. So, all the pretty wicker trellis, plastic trellis and small obelisks etc are perfectly strong enough to cope.

How to change the garden

As the plant dies in the autumn, it shrivels, and the stems are easy to remove without breaking the trellis.

Everlasting climbers

These are the perennial climbers, wicker or plastic trellis are simply not going to be able to cope with the weight or the vigour of these plants. You need to have sturdy trellis supported on solid and sturdy fixings to cope.

Large climbing plants get really heavy, flimsy trellis is not usually worth buying.

Take this picture. The rose exerts a huge stress force on the trellis as it grows out toward the sunshine. Even this sturdy trellis can be broken by the growth of the stems. A couple of short wall screws and rawlplugs are not going to last very long when the weight of the plant and the additional load caused by the wind and rain is added to the mix.

Fine for a sturdy wall trellis	*Best grown over a pergola*	*Usually too large for small gardens*
Annual Climbers	Clematis Montana	Rambling Roses
Most Clematis except Montana's	Campsis (Trumpet Vine)	Golden Hop (Humulus)
Medium Climbing Roses	Honeysuckle	Virginia Creeper (Parthenocissus)
Jasmine	Solanum (Potato Vine)	Ivy
	Larger Climbing Roses	Polygonatum (Mile a Minute)
	Wisteria	Hydrangea

In conclusion, if you plant anything that will last more than a few months, you need to buy the strongest trellis you can. If the plant says it will grow to ten feet tall in five years, then the trellis needs have at least ten feet for the plant to grow along. You can choose smaller trellis obviously, but then you will have to constantly reduce the size of the plant, be sure you have the time to devote to that ongoing battle.

Good trellis; wrong plant

All plants on trellis need training to the desired shape or tying in and this takes time. Some plants 'tie' themselves in and some plants can self-cling, which sounds great until you need to untangle them. Honeysuckle being a prime candidate for looking like a plate of overcooked spaghetti if you don't prune it properly.

If you intend to grow a plant up a trellis next to a fence or wall, then usually it's best to avoid the larger perennial climbers as they can quickly become a heavy unruly tangled mess that require extensive proper pruning every year to keep them in check.

Planting and Siting

All plants need three things to grow, food, water and light.

The problem with a trellis attached to a wall or fence is that usually once the trellis is attached, the plant ends up missing out on at least one of the vital elements.

Over time all plants will grow away from the fence and towards the light. If the trellis is fixed flush to the fence, the plant will always grow unevenly and will begin to suffer. Not enough light gets to the leaves lower down the trellis, the leaves fall off leaving bare stems.

Nothing can grow up here and actually look good.

When attaching a trellis to either a wall or a fence, the best way is to use a bracket. The trellis can be hung on the bracket, so if the fence needs a lick of paint, it is simply unhooked and laid flat. Plant the base of the plant as far away from the base of the fence as possible also.

In conclusion, always buy a bigger and stronger trellis, it won't disappoint, even though it costs a bit more.

What is dead space?

The key to making a design of any small garden successful is to minimize dead space. Dead space is created around, over and under an object. The space under a chair is dead space, the area around a table is dead space; you can't put anything there because you need access and so forth.

The garden needs to be thought of as a large 3-dimensional space into which objects are placed. Anything placed in the garden will form a cube corresponding to the space those objects use, the table and chairs will form the largest cube, hanging baskets will form a tall rectangle, pots will be smaller cubes and so forth.

Designing the garden is then a bit like 3-D Tetris, the cubes need arranging in the most efficient way trying to keep gaps to a minimum, because any gaps equate to unusable dead space in the garden. If you can get all the blocks to fit well together with few gaps, you will maximise the use of the small amount of space available.

Hanging baskets, why can't we think of something easier?

We have always had an obsession for hanging baskets and spend millions on these displays every year. Beautiful displays sing out the conquest of one's horticultural ability over the elements, however often, the result is never quite so spectacular.

Should we really keep on faithfully spending millions of pounds or is it time for a rethink?

Hanging baskets are not easy to look after!

Why? Well how many of you can identify with these issues:

See what I mean!

* The compost dries out so quickly you can't keep up with the watering requirement.

* You don't see most of the flowers as the basket is above your head.

* The flowers quickly fade, and you can never get the same intensity as in the garden centre.

* It's tricky to water properly, unless you put it on the floor first. Mostly the water just runs straight through.

* After a few days of summer sun, it all seems a bit shrivelled.

* The plants seem to get quickly smothered in bugs.

* After a few weeks, it's not clear if it's a feature or an eyesore, half the plants seem to have died, apart from the ivy, which has grown over everything else.

* Birds have pecked out the lining for nesting material, so the basket looks a bit tatty.

As a society, we are supposed to be trying to reduce, reuse and recycle more, it is better for us and the world at large. The problem though is that hanging baskets are sold as disposable. Garden centres would prefer you to throw the plants (and the basket) away. Gardening is already expensive, so why spend money to just throw something away, it does not make sense, surely it would be better spending money on plants that will last for several years instead.

As hanging baskets will still I suspect continue in popularity for many years; here are a few tips on how look after them more easily.

Firstly; don't hang them

Most of the problems associated with hanging baskets are created by hanging them up. Instead how about placing the baskets on top of pots or in pot stands. Place them on a log or pot and site them in the border. Placing the basket lower down allows you to water and feed more easily. You can even place the basket on the floor, just take off the hanging loops.

Plant your own; don't buy readymade baskets

Plants grow fastest and best if they are not competing for nutrients. Planting fewer plants in the basket ensures the plants have more space and soil to grow in, so they grow bigger and will look better for longer. In addition, because the baskets are not being hung; soil (which is heavier but more nutritious) can be mixed with the compost. This will help retain moisture for longer as well as providing a better growing environment for the plants.

Try to not use bedding plants

There are lots of plants that will grow in a basket well, that won't need throwing away at the end of the year. Bedding plants are disposable plants often have copious quantities of brightly coloured but mostly sterile flowers which provide no food for insects, none of which is very environmentally sensible. Bedding plants also tend to produce more as well as larger flowers than would naturally develop, all for our aesthetic delight of course. The result, the plants may look spectacular, but only if you follow a strict pampering and preening regime to keep these demanding plants performing. They are all high maintenance plants which is fine if you adore the pampering and preening regime, but it is a bit of a faff, if you haven't the time to. It is far better to use fewer demanding plants that thrive on a bit of neglect, there are loads to choose from, native wildflowers being one very obvious example.

Why not plant hanging baskets with plants that thrive in poor soils and sunny spots quite happily; like the native poppy or cornflowers instead.

Perhaps it is time for the fashions to change and we start to grow natural hanging baskets instead. Some of our wildflowers can be very beautiful and all can grow without human intervention, which makes them sound perfect for a hanging basket.

Remember, hanging baskets benefit the garden centre more than you.

The mark-up on planted hanging baskets is huge, nurseries and garden centres make a lot of money from selling planted baskets. However, more importantly, it is not in their financial interest for the baskets to survive. If they looked great all summer, we the consumer, would not

Use plants whose flowers won't wilt if you forget to water them every day like erigeron.

need to buy any more. As a result, baskets are crammed with plants, often too many for the size of basket. The plants all compete for water and available food in a multipurpose compost (used because it's lighter than soil) but it doesn't retain water very well, so the basket dries out quickly and the showiest flowers are invariably the first to suffer.

A granular plant food is normally added to the compost; however, these can only release enough food if the granules are wet but because the baskets drain quickly, these won't have enough time to dissolve. Now you may think this is being cynical and a tad unfair and maybe so, however ask yourself this; how many times have you had a stunning hanging basket display all summer? People can and do have the most beautiful displays if they have an utterly dedicated owner or have installed an automatic watering and feeding system.

So, there you have it, hanging baskets are great, if you like that sort of thing. But if you would like a lower maintenance garden; avoid using them.

Lawn rules

Lawns are an integral part of our gardens and as a nation we lavish millions on their upkeep and appearance. We all it seems, conform to the national standard that requires a verdant carpet of neatly trimmed stripes and manicured edges. In fact if any part of the lawn falls short of this standard, we find ourselves apologising for the poor state of our garden and succumb to society's collective pressure by spending time, money and effort spiking, rolling, feeding, weeding and raking in an attempt to rejuvenate and coax it back to life.

Why are there rules though, are they unbreakable and is it time for a rethink?

To understand why we are where we are, we need to go back to the 1950's and how the humble lawn became synonymous with your social standing. After World War Two there was a surge in housebuilding in this country, the Blitz had demolished many slum areas, providing the authorities the ability to start afresh. New homes were built with front gardens as well as back gardens, providing millions with their first ever space outside. After the chaos and destruction of the war, it is not surprising that the fashion

Why is this not a pretty lawn – it's certainly more interesting than plain green.

was for a neat, tidy and colourful garden, everyone was doing their bit to transform the destruction of the war years and show how much progress had been made. Now because many had not had gardens before, people turned to books to find out how to garden, the advice was simple; neat, straight and no daisies!

A flawless well-manicured lawn advertised to the neighbours that you were successful, diligent, hard-working and generally a 'good egg'. Neat perfect lawns became a badge of honour to show off with pride; but that was 70 years ago.

This convention has embedded itself into our collective gardening consciousness and we are still regaled with images that reinforce this ideology today. Perhaps after 70 years it is now time to rethink the rules on lawns, because let's face it, mowing the grass is without doubt the most time-consuming chore in most gardens.

In this new age of being more environmentally aware, we need to begin to regard a perfect lawn as a big green lifeless desert, only nice for us to walk on barefoot and not much else; so, here are a few challenges to the rules of the lawn:

- The lawn is only usually used to walk on, so would it really matter if there were a few daisies or clovers growing in the grass, as long as there weren't any prickly weeds lurking in the lawn, it would function just as well.

- Why does all the grass have to be cut to the same length? Could we not define a seating area by cutting the grass shorter and mowing a path through the lawn to get there?

- If we don't really walk or sit on the grass at all why have the grass mown short all the time; just because it's the 'done thing'?

- If the lawn always looks worn out, consider whether you are flogging a dead horse; would it be better to replace it with an alternative.

- Unless you need space for children to run around, do you really need to have all that space set aside for grass?

Tips for lawn design and shape:

We also need ensure the lawn that we have is not a chore that makes mowing more difficult.

- In a small garden make the lawn a regular proper shape, amoeba shaped lawns are difficult to mow.

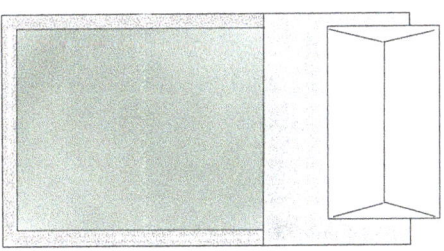

This is easy but boring.

- Before you shape the lawn, use the mower to see how easy it is to go 'around a corner' and check there is enough room to turn the mower round.

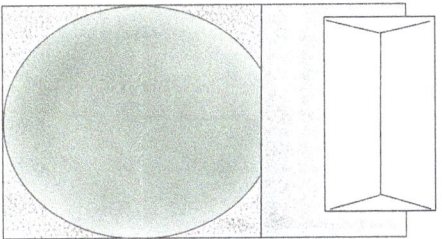

This is also easy but less boring.

- ❋ If you cut a grass path, create it in mower widths, one or two mowers wide.

- ❋ Shingle, gravel or decorative stones do NOT make good edges for lawns; ever.

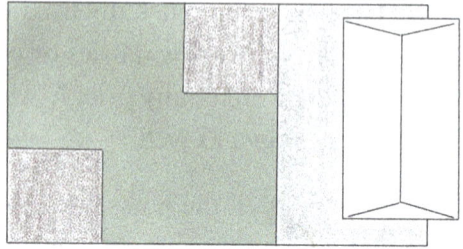
And this is still easy, but not at all boring.

- ❋ There is no point trying to grow grass under big trees, you don't see grass growing in a wood, only in a glade; fighting nature takes effort and time.

- ❋ Repairing lawns with fast growing lawn seed, OK that's fine, but grass is not intelligent, it won't know to only grow fast for the first few weeks, it will just grow fast forever.

The aim here is not to tell you how your lawn should be, just challenge the concept of what a perfect lawn is deemed to be.

Making a mess of a mulch

Every gardening book written usually extols the virtues of mulching and rightly so. A good mulch helps a gardener maintain the garden. So how does a mulch work and what could possibly go wrong with bunging 'stuff' on top of the soil?

Mulches work in two ways, the mulch stops sunlight beaming directly onto the soil, resulting in less evaporation and your soil stays wetter for longer. The absence of the sun on the soil prevents the germination of any seeds lying on the surface; which means fewer weeds growing in the borders. All of which is great, however there is a but! The mulch will work as it is supposed to only if sunlight can't reach the soil, which means the mulch needs to be at least 10cm deep. Anything less than that allows light through to the soil enabling all the weed seeds to merrily start growing. The weeds are then protected by the mulch itself; meaning they grow even more quickly. Mulches can be made of stones, shingle or

How to change the garden

This is supposed to be stopping the weeds growing, but it is not deep enough to stop sunlight hitting the ground.

fibrous material with or without the addition of a weed suppressing membrane underneath.

The problem starts because all gardens produce debris, and that debris sinks into the mulch making it difficult to clear up easily. This debris then breaks down to form little pockets of growing medium in the mulch; not unsurprisingly these then sprout weeds remarkably quickly.

The second problem with mulches is they can also become hiding places for lots of bugs and insects; some of which may be harmless and some may not, but because they are hidden, you can't see them until they have set upon your favourite Hosta overnight and eaten it. Now, I will always advocate encouraging a natural ecosystem in the garden because nature is much better at pest control than humans, but the addition of a mulch means those predators that happily eat the bad bugs can't see them either. The birds must go hunting in the mulch to find them, the result is your neat 10cm deep mulch gets flicked and kicked about all over the grass as the blackbirds dig their way through.

Power tools can't prune

Everyone loves a garden power tool and we use them to make gardening easier; well that is what the adverts show us anyway. Do they though, does wielding an electric hedge trimmer really make the gardening easier? Adverts show images of happy content gardeners merrily strimming immaculate lawns and cutting perfectly level hedges and certainly power tools will make some jobs quicker, but is quicker always better?

The 'art' of dome pruning!

If you have a large garden, long hedges, large lawns or tall trees, then power tools can be a bonus; if they are powerful enough for the job. In a small suburban garden, the battery powered garden tools often aren't worth the expense, much of the gardening work could be done just as easily by hand.

There are upsides to power tools though: speed, speed, and more speed.

But there are also downsides too: loss of precision, lack of power, clogging up, cleaning, cost, manoeuvrability, storage, and noise. Perhaps, before you head off to the DIY store this year, have a rethink, the plant may have outgrown the space it is in and there is a need to reduce its size, but do you really need a hedge trimmer?

Remember though, power tools can't prune, they can only do domes. You see them everywhere, small domes, tall domes, fat domes and thin domes, every garden seems to now have at least one dome.

Power tools just make the natural world look artificial.

Gardening is all about patience and being outside, if trimming the hedge takes a bit longer because it was hand cut with shears; would that really be so bad? Just think, of all that free exercise, less money has been spent, less storage is required and as for the garden being a gym, who could forget that scene from Poldark; scythe anyone!

Salt and pepper planting

Plants and gardens constantly change and evolve, plants die, and we buy new ones, consequently gardens very rarely get finished. This state of flux can all too easily dilute the original design idea and morph into a salt and pepper planting style; plants are dotted about all over the place. The border loses its framework, the plan that created the border has vanished and it all starts to resemble a bit of a dog's dinner.

'Pop it in planting' makes any design look bitty, instead have a theme and stick to it.

Avoiding the descent to salt and pepper planting just requires a little thought.

* Before you buy any plant, ask what role it will fulfil in the garden.
* Avoid impulse buying; unless the impulse purchase ticks the above point.
* Try not to buy single plants. For example, the mixed trays of six plants garden centre's sell by the gazillion, you get one each of everything, it's salt and pepper on a tray. Try to buy two or three of the same plant or if you buy one plant, split it into three before planting.
* Stick to a strong colour theme, the individual plants merge and mix, you get style from the drifts of colour working together rather than drifts of the same plants grouped together.

Be bold; size matters

Over the last few decades, garden sizes have been shrinking, new housing developments often now create gardens that are not much larger than the rooms inside the house. The mistake with a small garden however is to only use small sized plants. Now it's obvious that some plants are just going to get too big for a garden and shouldn't be used, but in terms of overall size, most plants will be fine.

Small gardens don't need smaller plants, they need smarter planting.

To create more impact in a small garden you need to think smart, think big and think multifunction:

* All plants must offer more than just pretty flowers. Scent, touch, taste or sound is equally important.

* No plant must be a light sucking monster; you do not want to just create another wall to look at, albeit a green one.

* Think height over width; use skinny self-supporting plants.

* Combine two or three plants to create one overall look, growing them in the same pot for example makes a more interesting and space saving display.

* It doesn't have to be a plant; you can use art or sculpture or amazing pots to create interest. Everything works together in one big performance.

Beware the vegetable garden

I absolutely approve of grow your own, but vegetable gardens are extremely labour intensive, so this section really is about growing vegetables without unwittingly creating a garden that takes up too much time.

So having been forewarned, if you know what you are committing too in having a vegetable garden, you can make better choices about the vegetables you would be able to grow; which hopefully results in the veg patch producing what you want and avoids you feeling either overwhelmed or disappointed.

The downside of vegetable gardens

* Vegetable gardens are not terrible attractive; for them to be efficient growing spaces, function trumps aesthetics.
* Most vegetables love growing in sunshine; so, in a small garden what wins, the sun lounger or the runner beans?
* Vegetables are maintenance heavy, if you want to eat your produce you have to stop everything else wanting to eat your produce.
* Netting to protect the veg from birds is not attractive in a small garden.
* Water; vegetables hate gardeners who forget to water regularly, they really sulk!
* Post-harvest, vegetable beds are not terribly attractive.
* To grow enough food to replace the weekly shop you need a lot of space.

All of this would seem to indicate that growing veg really is a no-no for many gardeners but it's not, it's just that there are easy veg to grow and needy veg to grow. I tried to grow veg, and even have a proper space for a veg garden, but was rubbish at it. I forgot or was too busy to water regularly so the spinach always bolted, the ants ate all the 'cut and come again' seed, carrots never materialized and where the onions disappeared too was a complete mystery. Despite supposedly being a gardener, I could never be enough of a devoted gardener to 'do' vegetables properly. The constant problem was aspiration superseding the time available.

The solution for me was to now only grow herbs and fruits that look after themselves, that my family actually enjoyed eating. The list reduced to Strawberries, Raspberries (the lazy autumn flowering variety), Courgette, Rhubarb, Garlic, Tomatoes, Asparagus and a small Fig tree. Apart from the tomatoes, I don't have to remember to water (much) and my vegetable patch does not require too much effort or time.

Vegetable gardens don't have to grow lots of different vegetables to be considered successful, what matters is that you enjoy the process of growing food to eat.

The advice is to be selective about what you choose to grow in the beginning, there is nothing worse than feeling a garden failure. Start with herbs, if you can't manage to keep a pot of basil on the windowsill looking healthy, perhaps a full blown veg patch is a step too far too soon?

In the glossary there is a list of needy vegetables pitfalls and problems. You can choose then which veg will work for you.

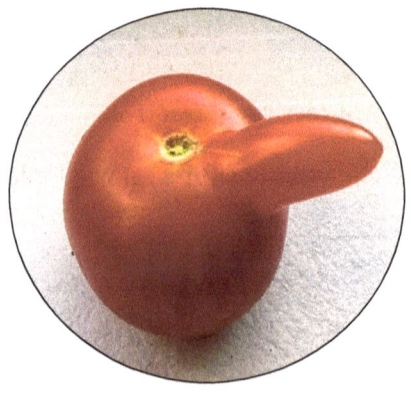

Home grown veg is far more fun than supermarket veg

How your garden can help save the world

Make no mistake, the small changes domestic gardeners collectively make impact the world around us, our back gardens are now vital resources for native wildlife, but gardening also has a dark side. Sadly, many common gardening practices exacerbate the destruction of our natural environment. You may think the garden is a natural green oasis but is that correct or are we kidding ourselves that having green is the same as being green?

How to have a better garden by gardening less

I do not strive for gardening perfection, it does not bother me if plants have a few nibble holes, they will grow back. I am not concerned if there are a few weeds in the lawn provided they are not prickly. If the sweet peas droop a bit and scramble over some plants; will I spend hours wondering how many more flower stalks I would have had if I had tied them in properly? No I won't.

Gardening books show you how to do things properly, to ensure the garden reaches its full potential where every plant flowers it's socks off, it all looks amazing and you are rightly proud of your efforts. The subliminal message however implies that by not doing all these things properly, your garden will be sub-par, a bit of a disappointment and you will have failed as a gardener. Nothing could be further from the truth.

The better approach is to think of the garden as a game, where there are several competing teams; the plants, unwanted plants, insects, unwanted insects, wildlife big or small and humans. The gardener's role is simply to act as the referee. Your role is to ensure all the competing teams play fairly and no one team gains an upper hand, it is a light touch approach to gardening, there to ensure the game continues for everyone. It is not about the result; humans 1: the environment 0, is not a desirable outcome. Your role is to oversee this game for a while before you hand the game onto someone else.

This approach to gardening really is liberating, because the primary purpose is about balance. If no team gains the upper hand, the game is fair, and all the players benefit.

Tiny eggs on a leaf covered in a dew drop.

If one team starts getting the upper hand, for example the roses are suddenly decimated by bad bugs with aphids sucking the life out of them. It is dealt with by considering why the aphids are attacking the roses. How have they got the upper hand in the game? Previously the chemical cupboard may have been opened; but this would then be unfair for the good bugs team because they'll all be killed too.

Instead you need act as referee; one team has an unfair advantage, there is an imbalance, which needs your intervention. Restoring the equilibrium could be achieved by attracting more bug hunters by planting more insect friendly flowers, you could squash the aphids by hand (glass of wine in one hand, glove on the other hand approach . . .), pop up a bird feeder to attract small birds in right next to the affected plants etc.

The key point being, the remedy does not have to be instant, you do not need to destroy all life to just get rid of the aphids. Stopping this relentless drive for perfection releases every gardener from much of the burden of gardening, your ethos is instead to create an environment you enjoy in partnership with the world outside.

The game of the garden is a long one, your garden will outlive you

Buying the wrong sort of plant

How you choose to purchase plants and what you choose to buy can also create problems, not only for you but also for the environment. Every plant you buy should be thought through, not just in terms of whether it is the right plant for your garden, but also whether that plant comes with its own hefty carbon footprint.

Plant are sold like sweeties in an aisle and all with tempting 'buy me now' offers.

Horticulture is a business, the aim is to grow plants to sell, it uses a low margin, high volume business model. To encourage customers to buy, plants are forced into producing flowers, the more flowers on show, the more plants are sold. Customers are deluged with tempting offers, plants of the week promotions, plants are combined with pots, baskets and planters not to make your life easier, but to add value and increase profit margins.

Sales and turnover are key, the industry needs customers to buy the plants they grow. Plants are produced cheaply and quickly, the more you buy, the more plants are grown which then must be sold, and so the merry go round continues.

The issue is that these bargain bucket plants are not designed to last; they are grown and sold as quick fixes to be disposed of at the end of the season. This type of business model that promotes the selling of disposability is increasingly harder to justify. Collectively we all need to reduce consumption, it simply makes little sense to keep producing and then buying plants in this way.

Bedding plants, single season plant displays, are the plastic bottles of the plant world. Although the plants can be composted and won't add to the global rubbish pile, it is not this that causes the problem. All these plants are grown in a factory farmed environments and use huge quantities of artificial light, heat, space and water just to produce plants that are designed to be thrown away after a few months. This is neither cost effective for gardeners nor is it particularly green. By the way, there is an alternative to the curse of the super-fast colourful bedding plant however and that is to buy bulbs instead.

Garden Centre, DIY store or Plant Nursery?

Garden Centres are plant supermarkets whereas Plant Nurseries are the growers of plants and there are advantages and disadvantages using both:

Arguably garden centres and DIY stores are convenient places to source plants, they offer a wide choice as well as being a place to wander about and have a coffee or a bite to eat; they are designed to make your shopping experience a pleasure. However, these supermarkets are less worried about what you are buying, just that you are buying something. Garden Centres commission growers to produce huge volumes of certain types of plants (and have committed to buy those plants) so the focus is on selling those plants and not selling you the right plants for your garden. If the plants have a relatively short garden life, then all the better as that generates repeat sales and so the cycle continues.

Nurseries usually only sell plants, but you may not find all the plants you are looking for in one place, but online shopping has made searching for plants much easier. Although less of a one stop shop, the plants nurseries sell have usually been grown in the UK in their entirety and are not shipped in from the continent or flown in from the Far East. The carbon footprint (in the resources used in making the plant available to buy) can be much less and the plants are well acclimatised to our weather, so are usually more robust once planted in your garden.

Garden Centres / DIY Stores	*Plant Nursery*
Usually these are larger companies with several retails outlets and may also grow plants for their group of companies	Tend to be smaller individually owned or family firms
Tend to buy only from large scale commercial growers and supply companies only	Sell plants direct from the nursery via online sales, plant shows and fairs. May supply garden centres
More interested in stocking plants with a fast turnover, quick to set flower and easy to sell	Usually will specialise in growing certain types of plants only
High volume: low margin sales	These are plant specialists and can offer expert advice
Provides a supermarket style shopping experience	Less variety of produce on sale, but offer a wider selection of their specialty plants instead
Convenient	The internet has now made buying from nurseries far easier
Lots of seasonal plants on offer, many are imported from overseas.	Plants from nurseries have often been grown on-site so are fully acclimatised

It boils down to this, if you are in a garden centre and you saw two identical plants, one cost £8.49 and was flown in from Thailand last week the other £9.95 but was delivered from a local plant nursery; which would you choose to buy?

Why buying from a garden centre may not be very 'green'?

Now whilst I don't want to cast garden centres as demonic institutions hell bent on saturating the world with brightly coloured bedding plants pre-planted in gaudy coloured plastic pots; as there are very many wonderful garden centres around. It is becoming more important to be more discerning when purchasing plants.

Changes in our food buying habits are already forcing food supermarkets to introduce wonky veg and plastic free aisles. There is no reason we cannot create change in the current horticultural sales model either.

Food for thought

* Ask what does the label 'Grown in the UK' really mean? It has been grown in the UK from seed to sale or just imported a few weeks ago to finish off growing here?

Plants don't flower as well as this without extra help.

* Is the new plant variety on display, buzzing with bees or butterflies or do they fly right on past?

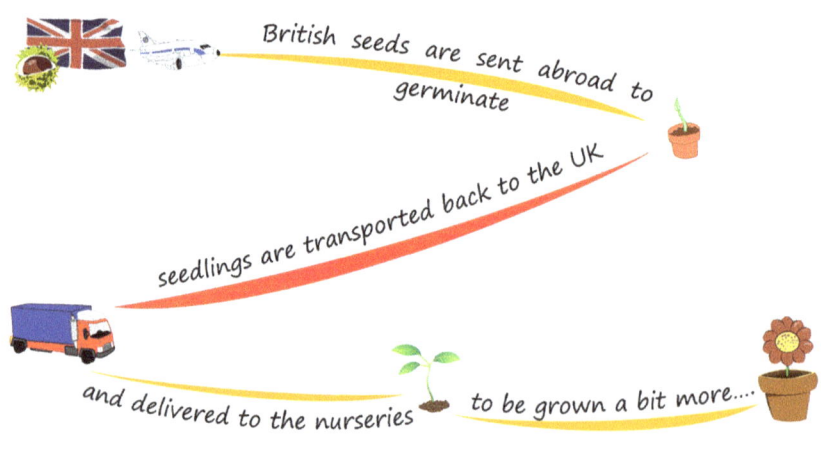

British seeds are sent abroad to germinate

seedlings are transported back to the UK

and delivered to the nurseries to be grown a bit more....

Then they can be sold to you as....

grown in Britain!

* Ask what you will do with the plastic pot the plant was sold in?
* The hanging basket liner, is it recyclable?
* How much heat, light, water and resources has that plant used up being forced into flower months before it would naturally?
* How will planting these bedding flowers improve the garden and how long for?
* Is the 'Miracle 7-day speedy green lawn' restorer necessary?

All companies sell and produce more of their products that sell well. If we purchase more of the plants that do good, less of the artificial chemicals that do harm and buy less of the produce designed to last a few weeks; the world of horticulture will respond.

It is time to ensure our green spaces really are green places.

Buying plants for the first time

Horticulture doesn't make buying plants easy for inexperienced gardeners, although plants may well be conveniently grouped together by type; climbers, perennials, herbs, grasses, roses, etc., which helps to a point, but when was the last time you saw a border only planted with climbers or a garden that contained nothing but roses, it just doesn't happen. As a result, choosing plants to combine in a border is hard if you aren't sure if a Hosta will grow well next to a Helenium for example.

Plants may look spectacular in the garden centre, but that's only because they have been grown by experts in perfect conditions!

So, here is our first timers guide to buying plants.

- Never ever impulse buy; it's too easy to acquire an expensive mistake.
- Always buy smaller plants over bigger specimens; they are easier to get growing once planted.
- Buy out of season; it's cheaper.
- Check the Size in Five, will the plant still fit the available space in five years' time?
- Buy the plant if it is more than just a 'pretty face', buy it because it smells lovely or has soft tactile leaves also. It must charm more than just one of your senses.
- Big showy flowers equals more gardening effort.
- Is it insect friendly; are there any bees or insects buzzing about the flowers?
- Read the label properly, don't become a right plant; wrong place expert.
- Each plant fills a space in the garden, but what is the job description for that space?

Which means, whenever you are going to get plants for the garden, you need to think in terms of the space the plant needs to fill, and you need to know how big the plant will ultimately get. It is important to know before planting, that the plant won't outgrow the allotted space.

In a small garden you want to get most enjoyment for your money (plants are expensive after all) so a good test is the senses test.

Buy a plant not just because it looks pretty, buy it because it looks pretty BUT it also smells nice, it is nice to touch, you can taste it or it makes a nice sound in a breeze, that way the plant will hold your interest in the garden more than one with just pretty flowers. You can also choose to only buy plants that attract insects, bees, and butterflies, again, the plant is more interesting to watch in the garden.

In choosing plants using a job description, you ensure you minimise the risk of right plant wrong place, by matching what you need the plant to do, you are less likely to plant a mistake.

However, you do need know what the plant descriptions on the labels really mean.

Plant labels and what they really mean ...

Understanding what's on a plant label is now thankfully easier as the horticultural industry has standardised most labels to show pictograms of information which are straightforward and simple to understand. The problem is in the description of the plant, it's not what is written; it is what's not been written. Nurseries and garden centres want you to buy their plants, so not surprisingly the plant descriptions will always highlight the plus points, however, as plant buyers there are some clues in the plant descriptions you would do well to heed!

What the label says	But what it really means!
Architectural	Thorns, spikes and pokey bits
Spreads slowly via underground roots	Will pop up 'miles' from where you planted it; but not so fast as you can't control it
Spreads via underground roots	Will pop up 'miles' from where you planted it as soon as you turn your back
Prone to suckering	Even worse than spreads via underground ...
Vigorous ...	Never stops growing
Good for naturalising	Is not good in a small garden!
Self-seeds	Think about what's downwind; these seeds will pop up everywhere
May need staking	Will fall over at the slightest puff of wind and face-plant after heavy rain
Fast-growing	Fast-growing now and forever, buy some secateurs!

Good for hedging	*Grows thick and fast*
Aphids may be a problem…	*This is every bugs favourite dinner*
Self-clinging climber	*Will happily grow up the wall and under your roof tiles if allowed*
New this year	*Created by a plant nursery for human enjoyment only, may be useless for a bee*
New variety	*See above*
Bears fruit	*Beware wasp attracting big ripe fruit 'bombs'*
Attractive seed pods	*But what about the unattractive spent seed pods, where will you put those?*
Amazingly large leaves	*Amazingly large amounts of leaf debris in winter*
Forms large clumps	*Will need industrial digging to lift and divide the clump every two or three years*
Evergreen	*Drops some of its leaves in summer*
Deciduous	*Drops all its leaves anytime from the autumn onwards*
Trailing	*Liable to tangle everywhere and trip you up*
Spectacular	*Is possibly a short-lived plant; parties hard and dies young.*
Good for dry shade	*Don't plant anywhere else or it will take over the garden*

New plant varieties; good or bad?

Every year at all the major flower shows hundreds of new varieties of plant are introduced to the general public which is lovely, however there is a but; and that is whether these new varieties are any good for your garden.

Horticultural growers over many decades have created flowers with increasingly exotic petal shapes and colour combinations; the problem though, is who are these new flowers designed to please?

It may be bold and bright for us, but for a bee; many modern blooms don't even look like flowers

Flowers evolved for one purpose only and that was to attract pollinators so seed could be set, and the plant could ensure its survival.

Not any more though, many of the new hybrid plant varieties being developed and sold in garden centres are now so 'developed' the flowers themselves offer nothing by way of pollen or nectar at all. Why, because pollen and nectar are not important to us, the selective breeding of plants has in many cases rendered this function of the flower obsolete, in its place are bigger, brighter and more complex petals. If these plants have no purpose other than to look pretty, can these hybrids even be thought of as flowers at all?

If the plants provide no food for foraging bees or insects, they do no good, so why not just have artificial flowers in the garden instead? Clearly most of us would recoil at the idea of a garden full of plastic flowers, but these overly bred/hybridised barren flowers are as useful to a bee as a plastic plant. So why not subscribe to the 'my garden can help save the world' philosophy right from the start and only use flowers that are useful to bees and butterflies and all other pollinators.

Borage, however, is a very bee-friendly flower

BEE-ing more friendly

Plants evolved flowers for one purpose and one purpose only; which is to help disperse pollen. Plants relied on insects to transport pollen between flowers ensuring the species reproduced. The reward to the insect for carrying out this task was nectar; the key point being that both plant and insect benefitted.

Bees also see in ultraviolet light, what we see of a flower and what a bee sees are entirely different; so many of the new plant varieties on show are utterly invisible to a bee. Incidentally if you want to see some truly wonderful photographs taken from a bee's perspective, have a look at Craig Burrows photography website (cpburrows.com), the images are stunning.

Breeding flowers that don't attract foraging insects, bees, or insects is evolutionary suicide, but there is something you can do. Only buy plants that are attractive to butterflies or bees, you may no longer have the biggest, boldest or showiest blooms, but you will without question have the best flowers.

To provide a garden with more bee friendly flowers:

* Choose open flowers, so avoid doubles and overly cultivated blooms.
* Avoid using bedding plants.
* Choose more natural looking colours, petal shapes and flower sizes.
* Buy plants that flower in every season.
* Use some native wildflowers in the borders too.

Why show gardens should never be copied

Show Gardens are fantastic, they represent all that is innovative, stunning (expensive), and exciting and the gardening public flock to see these gardens at the world's biggest and best flower shows. We are wowed at every turn by picture perfect plant paradises packed full of colour, scent and cool stuff and it's great. Then once home, all bar a very select few expert gardeners, most of us will wander out into our own little patches of planting imperfection and let out a slightly deflated sigh because our gardens just don't look anything like the ones in the shows. Should we really feel such disappointment that our efforts fall way short of the standards set in a show garden?

No of course we shouldn't.

Major garden shows are just that; they are shows.

The aim of a show is to impress and in order to do that you need to work at superhuman levels to elevate the garden and create a showstopping performance. In just the same way as a fashion show, all the elements have been meticulously selected, preened, pressed, powdered, pampered and exhibited; all for a small moment in time; but for that moment it must be fantastic.

To try to maintain that level of perfection for the whole year is simply not possible. One could also argue that it is not environmentally sensible either. For example, to ensure all the flowers bloom at the right time, heat, light, fertiliser and refrigerators are used to achieve perfection. Plants are rehoused in polytunnels, sprayed with insecticide and other pest control methods to appear perfect. In a show garden that is fine, but we should not then try to emulate this at home nor indeed regard any inability to recreate it as a failure on our part.

Show gardens should really be viewed as the catwalk fashion model of the horticultural world, stunning eye-candy to admire from a distance, but not to copy at home.

Gardens aren't just for us

One of life's simplest pleasures is to sit in a garden on a warm sunny day and watch the garden hum with activity. Gardens that are created solely with the purpose of pleasing humans are missing the whole point of gardening. Creating a garden that provides a nice place to sit that also encourages and nurtures nature is the best of both worlds.

Gardens aren't separate from nature they are part of the natural world, the only difference between wild nature and domestic nature is a fence.

It is still the case though that much of the gardening advice provided by the garden media deals with how to do things properly, how to deal with pestilence and disease. The underlying inference being that if these things are not done, the garden won't be perfect and won't put on a good show. This approach though makes gardening an extremely labour-intensive exercise as perfection takes time. So, does not having the time to devote to being a committed gardener, mean that you are condemned to either a rubbish looking garden because you don't have the time or that you should opt for a non-garden, wall to wall artificial turf with a couple of plastic pot plants on show; absolutely not!

This is the show you need the garden to put on for you.

The problem is not that your garden isn't good enough, it's that the gardening rules are outdated. It is time to change the idea of what a great garden is, by changing the idea of what it means to put on a 'show'. Why cannot the show element of the garden be the benefit the garden provides to wildlife.

A garden which caters for us and all native wildlife is beautiful and watching the butterflies' flit about is a darn sight more interesting than admiring how upright the delphiniums are!

Spray less

Don't fill the garden with plants that require lots of attention and spraying to look good. Chemicals aren't clever, they just kill everything, but if you choose fewer demanding plants, you won't need to spray. Ditch the plant divas and plant something more self-sufficient instead.

Have fewer but deeper borders

Quality always supersedes quantity, one wide deep border that has a balanced planting scheme not only looks better it also provides a more natural habitat for wildlife. It will have both nesting places for the birds and hiding places for hedgehogs or lizards.

Compost your food and garden waste

In the not too distant future, we are all going to be expected to recycle our food waste and not simply chuck it in the bin. I expect some bright spark will find a way to weigh household waste so that councils can charge households by the kilogram. The era of smart waste will soon be upon us; so why not get ahead of the curve. There are easy ways to compost household food waste and turn it into life giving nutrients for your garden, from Bokashi bins in the kitchen to Hot bins on the patio, all of us will need to make changes to our food disposal habits. All my food waste goes back onto my garden. I only throw out one bin bag of rubbish per week (in a family of five), which is only filled with non-recyclable plastic waste (sadly); but it weighs nothing. I could do more, but if I can do it, so can you.

Ecosystems can be large and also small.

But what if you only have a small garden!

You can still make a difference by adding a few easy features. You'd be surprised at what you can do with even the smallest of spaces. Even if you've just got a border or a small patch of patio, there are still things you can do.

* Be a little less tidy, just a little unkempt area will attract lots of life.

* Don't spray, or if you must, use it as a last resort and use an environmentally friendly one.

* Have an insect hotel, bird box, bat box or hedgehog house.

- Only buy plants that are good for bees and insects.
- Have one plant that flowers in winter.
- Cut a hedgehog hole in the fence.
- Plant bulbs instead of bedding plants.

If you can create a garden that hums with life you also help yourself, Nature balances out the volume of pests with the volume of predators, which means you don't get overrun with bugs that chomp your favourite flowers. You have helped the planet by being just a little more nature aware in the garden, it really is a win-win situation.

You don't need a power tool for everything

Power tools don't necessarily make gardening easier, as has already been said earlier, power tools only make gardening faster. If their benefit is just speed, should we be reconsidering how much we rely on these tools also.

There is now a tool for everything, but we don't really need a tool for everything, do we? So, whilst I am not advocating everyone resort to shears and a bow saw, manual gardening is often the better approach. If we can get past the need for speed, perhaps we can recapture the precision of our own human power tool, the arm. If nothing else, clipping the hedge is a great free work out! Buying a product you don't need means resources are used that didn't need to be. Globally we all need to cut our consumption, we need to stop buying stuff; perhaps this is the question we should always be asking?

'Do I need it or just want it?'

OK, it might not be the world's greatest garden but ...

I hope that having now read this book and thank you by the way, some of your previously held perceptions of gardening have changed and I have challenged your understanding of what being a gardener and 'doing the gardening' means.

The whole premise of this book has been to try and offer simple solutions to many of the gardening dilemmas inexperienced (or unenthusiastic) garden owners have, so that gardening is made easier and the garden is a more enjoyable place to be.

The garden you have should allow you the time and space to be outside without being reminded of the chores that need doing or make you feel you aren't a proper gardener because you aren't gardening in a textbook fashion.

I sincerely hope that some of the methods I have used to change the layout of a garden or rework garden borders have provided you with not only the knowledge but also the confidence to get out in your garden and have a go at making your garden a place you want to be in.

Gardening has no magic formula or quick fix guide to creating that perfect outdoor space but understanding how and why problems occur that prevent you from enjoying the garden is important. If you avoid getting it wrong, then you must be getting it right. It may not be 100% perfect, but no garden ever is, if however, your garden is 80% perfect, I'll bet you enjoy being in it a whole lot more than you do right now.

OK, it might not be the world's greatest garden but ...   131

The established rules by which our gardening prowess have traditionally been judged now need updating and changing. Gardeners should not feel shackled by convention or hemmed in by the ideal standards that currently apply and by not having to adhere to accepted gardening standards means anyone can create and enjoy their garden. The only box that needs ticking is that the garden works for you, is easily maintained by you to your standards and that you enjoy sitting in the space you have created.

Having a garden should also never be regarded as a battle whereby you are in a seemingly never-ending fight against plant munching foes, the elements, gravity, disease and so forth to try and maintain the garden in a properly managed state. Gardening is not a contest between you and the world outside; there is no world outside, there is only the world we share.

Creating a garden that benefits you and benefits the world is a better and more sustainable approach. Your garden really can help save the world.

Once illuminated we see our world as it truly is; beautiful but fragile

Useful stuff to know about plants

'Needy' Vegetables

Growing fruit and vegetables takes time and commitment, it doesn't mean you need to garden the veg patch every day, but if the intention is to grow enough produce to supplement your diet or to replace the need to buy certain vegetables, you arc going to have to garden more. The key to getting a good crop is regular attention, forgetting to water the tomatoes for a day or two will not kill the plant, but it will affect the volume of tomatoes produced, tending to the vegetables needs to become part of your routine. There are some vegetables however whose needs are greater than others; some vegetable require a large space in which to grow whilst other will sulk if they miss out on their daily water.

All fruit bearing plants love plenty of sunshine, food and water, so strawberry, raspberry, blueberry, (anything with ... berry in the name) requires regular watering to ripen the fruits as well as protection from all those animals that love eating the fruits just as much as you do.

Like any part of gardening, if you are happy and committed to knowing what will be needed to produce the result you want; the business of gardening does not feel such of a chore; it's only when aspiration and ability are out of synch, the result is usually disappointment.

Useful stuff to know about plants

Vegetable / Fruit	Biggest 'need'
Artichoke	Space and lots of water
Asparagus	Water, space and patience
Aubergine (Eggplant)	Water and space
Beans	Water and a sacrificial companion planting to lure away blackfly
Beetroot	Are not 'needy'
Broccoli	Space
Brussel Sprouts	Space
Cabbage	Space and protection from pigeons
Capsicum (peppers)	Always hungry, always thirsty
Carrots	Are not 'needy'
Celeriac	Always thirsty
Celery	Always thirsty
Courgette (Zucchini)	Space and water
Cucumber	A greenhouse and lots of water
Fennel	Always thirsty
Leeks	Are not 'needy'
Lettuce	Never forget to water and have a repeat sowing cycle
Marrow	Lots of space
Mushrooms	A dark cupboard
Onions	Are not 'needy'
Parsnips	Are not 'needy'
Peas	Water and lots of space if you want more than just a handful
Potatoes	Space
Pumpkin	Lots of space, water and food
Radish	Are not 'needy'
Shallots	Are not 'needy'
Swede	Water
Sweetcorn	Space
Tomatoes	Always hungry, always thirsty
Turnips	Are not 'needy'

Garlic Spray recipe

Garlic spray is an effective bug munching repellent. It won't guarantee being 100% effective, but neither does any other chemical spray; but this one is completely safe for the environment.

Ingredients:

    1 whole garlic bulb.

    A squirt of environmentally friendly washing up liquid or soap (optional).

    1 litre of water.

    1 spray dispenser bottle.

This is so simple, simply blitz up the garlic in a mixer or by hand and mix with the water. Leave it to infuse for a few hours or overnight, then strain the liquid into the spray dispenser.

Add a squirt of liquid soap this helps to coat the leaves a little better, but it can be left out.

Then spray on your plants.

Regular spraying is needed to be an effective deterrent; but apparently lots of bugs, snails and slugs don't like the taste of garlic, so they will head off to the nearest garden that doesn't spray garlic everywhere!

and who knows, perhaps predators will prefer garlic flavoured snails even more!

Plants that fight back!

Poisonous	Spikes, Thorns or Prickles	Can be an Irritant	Can be an Irritant
Aconitum (kills)	Agave	Abutilon	Lobelia
Actea (poisonous berries)	Berberis	Alstroemeria	Narcissus
Brugmansia (kills)	Chaemoneles	Arisaema	Oleander
Colchicum (Autumn Crocus)	Citrus	Arum	Ornithogalum
Convallaria (Lily of the Valley)	Cratageus	Asparagus	Parthenosissus
Daffodil	Echinops	Capsicum	Ranunculus
Delphinium	Eryngium	Chyrsanthemum	Rhamnus
Digitalis (Foxgloves)	Gunnera	Dicentra	Rhus
Hydrangea	Holly (Ilex)	Dictamnus	Ruta
Laburnum (deadly seeds)	Humulus	Echium	Tulips
Oleander (toxic smoke)	Mahonia	Euphorbia	Zantedeschia
Rhododendron	Pyracantha	Hedera (Ivy)	
Ricinus (kills)	Raspberry	Hellebores	
Robinia	Roses	Hyacinth	
Sophora	Rubus	Iris	

These widely available garden plants are expert at getting their own back. All have thorns, poisons or can irritate; gardening gloves are an essential when handling any of these.

Plants that will misbehave if allowed!

This is the section that probably should be titled 'why didn't the plant label say that', it's what you wished you'd known before installing the plant in your garden.

These are the worst offenders given the wrong place in a garden, although given the right place they can be wonderful plants to have. Self-seed experts for example should never be planted upwind of a patio and those that spread via underground roots need planting well away from paths or paving.

Plants that thrive in tough conditions will quickly take over any border where the conditions are easier to grow, so make sure you only plant these in the tough spaces, where they excel at becoming wonderful weed suppressing friends.

Plant at leisure ... regret forever; in other words, if you have a small garden think hard before planting any of the following plants.

Fennel is lovely but it does spread everywhere if allowed!

Useful stuff to know about plants

Procreators
All Grasses
Aquilegia
Borage
Briza
Fennel
Forget me Not
Honesty
Lychnis
Oenertha
Nigella
Poppy

Speed Spreaders
Allium Triquetium
Allium Sphaerocephalon
Bluebells
Convolvulus
Crocosmia (some not all)
Galium Oderatum
Iris Foetissima
Lily of the Valley
Physalis
Pulmonaria
Valerian

Escape Artists
Campsis
Ivy
Moss Rose
Rhus
Susa (Bamboo)

Forget Me Not self-seeds everywhere but is rather lovely.

Hard to get rid of
Anemone japonica
Buddleja
Eucalyptus
Fuchsia (perennial)
Papaver
Persicaria

Triffids!
Clematis Montana
Comfrey
Fallopia
Lamium
Pachysandra
Polygonum

Attention Seekers
All Bedding Plants
Dahlias
Delphiniums
Gladioli
Hanging Baskets
Lily

Whereas Buddleia although very beautiful grows fast and is tough to get rid of.

Creating your plant wardrobe

The idea behind creating the concept of a plant wardrobe is its familiarity. We all understand how to combine clothes, assigning clothes to types of plants makes it easier to work out how to plan a border. The border plan is then created using the boxes method described. This is not a method to create a border worthy of inclusion in the Chelsea Flower Show, but it will look a whole lot better than planting a mixed box of bedding, a couple of conifers and hoping for the best! The beauty of having your own wardrobe though is that you can decide what each plant does, it is your wardrobe. So, yours for example, could look something like this:

Sarcococca flowers in winter.

Goes with Everything	*Jeans and Jumpers*	*Special Occasion*	*Best Accessories*	*Favourite Tops*
Acer	Aucuba	Abutilon	Alliums	Agapanthus
Buxus	Azalea	Bamboo	Tulips	Campanula
Cotinus	Camellia	Berberis	Balls or Spheres	Dianthus
Grasses	Carex	Callicarpa	Anything Orange	Gaura
Hebe	Cornus	Callistemon	Mirrors	Geum
Hosta	Dicentra	Cimicifuga	Tall Pots	Paeony
Hydrangea	Escallonia	Daphne	Solar Lights	Primrose
Ligustrum	Euphorbia	Garrya		Salvia
Osmanthus	Fatsia	Hamamellis		Viola
Philadelphus	Hosta	Hibiscus		
Pittosporum	Lavender	Lavatera		
Roses	Magnolia	Magnolia		
Sarcococca	Pieris	Monarda		
Spirea	Rhododendron	Myrtus		
Syringa				

Useful stuff to know about plants 139

What a plant does best

Plants do different things, so another useful method to help decide which plants you would like to use in a garden is to choose a solely by what it does best.

Plants that won't flop over (much)

Acer	Achillea	Agapanthus	Agastache	Anemone
Canna	Cornus	Crocosmia	Dierama	Digitalis
Echinops	Eremurus	Eryngium	Euphorbia	Hemerocallis
Hydrangea	Iris	Kniphofia	Lychnis	Miscanthus
Molinia	Pennisetum	Penstemon	Persicaria	Phormium
Phyllostachys	Rosemary	Rudbeckia	Salvia	Sambucus
Sanguisorba	Sarcococca	Schizostylis	Stipa	Sisyrinchium
Thalictrum	Verbascum	Verbena	Viburnum	Zantedeschia

'Look at Me' Plants

Abutilon	Acanthus	Akebia	Anemone Jap'ica	Astrantia
Callistemon	Canna	Choiysa	Cimicifuga	Circium
Crambe	Crocosmia	Crocus	Cyclamen	Dahlia
Dierama	Echinops	Elymus	Eryngium	Eupatorium
Euphorbia	Fatsia	Hakonechloa	Hellebore	Heuchera
Hosta	Hydrangea	Imperata	Iris	Ligularia
Lychnis	Magnolia	Mahonia	Millium	Ophiopogon
Paeony	Perovskia	Phormium	Rhododendron	Rudbeckia
Sanguisorba	Scabiosa	Sophora	Tulips	Zantedeschia

140   I want to like my garden

Loud and proud flowers

Achillea	*Agapanthus*	*Agastache*	*Artemesia*	*Camassia*
Canna	*Cirsium*	*Cotinus*	*Crocosmia*	*Dianthus*
Emilia	*Escholtzia*	*Genista*	*Geranium*	*Geum*
Helenium	*Hemerocallis*	*Heuchera*	*Imperata Rubra*	*Iris*
Knautia	*Kniphophia*	*Ligularia*	*Linum*	*Lychnis*
Ophiopogon	*Paeony*	*Papaver*	*Persicaria*	*Photinia*
Potentilla	*Rudbeckia*	*Salvia*	*Scabiosa*	*Schizostylis*
Sedum	*Sophora*	*Tulip*	*Verbena*	

Cooler colours and pastel shades

Abelia	*Abutilon*	*Achillea*	*Allium*	*Amsonia*
Aquilegia	*Armeria*	*Astrantia*	*Bergenia*	*Campanula*
Catananche	*Clematis*	*Coreopsis*	*Dianthus*	*Diascia*
Dicentra	*Dierama*	*Foxglove*	*Gaura*	*Gypsophilia*
Hebe	*Hellebore*	*Hosta*	*Leucanthemum*	*Lysimachia*
Nemesia	*Nepeta*	*Ornithogalum*	*Papaver*	*Penstemon*
Physotegia	*Potentilla*	*Rosemary*	*Scabiosa*	*Sisyrinchium*

Echinacea and Sedum, not only very pretty, but bee friendly too.

Plants to touch

Achillea	Ammi Majus	Alchemilla	Artemesia	Amsonia
Aquilegia	Artemesia	Carex	Cosmos	Deschampsia
Dicentra	Dierama	Dill	Dryopteris	Elymus
Fennel	Gaura	Grasses	Gypsophilia	Hakonechloa
Lavender	Lychnis	Molinia	Miscanthus	Nepeta
Orlaya	Pennisetum	Perovskia	Stachys	Stipa

Happy flowers

Aquilegia	Armeria	Bluebells	Borage	Camassia
Campanula	Celandine	Convallaria	Cosmos	Crocus
Cyclamen	Dianthus	Diascia	Emilia	Escholtzia
Frittilaria	Geum	Gladioli	Linum	Lychnis
Narcissus	Papaver	Potentilla	Primula	Ranunculus
Rhododendron	Salvia	Tulips	Verbena	Viburnum

Escholtzia; a happy flower in a happy colour.

Plants that aren't always green

Acer	Canna	Carex	Choiysa	Cimicifuga
Convolvulus	Cornus	Cotinus	Elymus	Eryngium
Eupatorium	Fennel	Hakonechloa	Hebe	Heuchera
Hosta	Imperata Rubra	Libertia	Lychnis	Millium
Ophiopogon	Phormium	Pittosporum	Poa	Rue
Salix	Sambucus	Sedum		

Plants that dance in the breeze

Agrostis	Allium	Ammi Majus	Aquilegia	Campanula
Carex	Cimicifuga	Clematis	Cosmos	Deschampsia
Dierama	Dill	Eremurus	Fennel	Foxgloves
Galax	Gaura	Gypsophilia	Miscanthus	Molinia
Orlaya G'flora	Pennisetum	Perovskia	Phyllostachys	Poa

Plants that are nice to smell

Abelia	Agastache	Artemesia	Bluebell	Buddleja
Choisya	Daphne	Hamamelis	Lavender	Mahonia
Myrtle	Narcissus	Nemesia	Nepeta	Olearia
Perovskia	Philadelphus	Rhododendron	Rosemary	Salvia
Sarcococca	Sweet Pea	Syringa	Viburnum	

Plants every garden should find space for

Achillea	Allium	Aquilegia	Crocus	Cyclamen
Daphne	Dryopteris	Foxglove	Geranium	Geum
Hellebore	Heuchera	Iris	Lavender	Miscanthus
Narcissus	Ophiopogon	Paeony	Primula	Rosemary
Sarcococca	Sedum	Stipa	Tulip	Verbena

Useful stuff to know about plants 143

Messy trees and untidy plants

Shrubs or small trees that make a mess

Abutilon	Amelanchier	Apple Tree	Birch	Catalpa
Cherries	Cornus	Crab Apple	Elderflower	Eucalyptus
Fatsia	Fig	Garrya	Gunnera	Hornbeam
Hydrangea	Liquidambar	Mulberry	Palms	Pine
Plum	Parthenosissus	Pyracantha	Willow	Wisteria

Fast growing plants

Campsis	Clematis	Cornus	Elderflower	Eucalyptus
Fig	Gunnera	Hollyhock	Honeysuckle	Humulus
Hydrangea	Ivy	Jasmine	Leylandii	Persicaria
Philadelphus	Privet	Rhododendron	Rhus	Tropaeolum
Willow	Wisteria			

Plants that never look very neat

Buddleja	Campsis	Clematis	Comfrey	Cotoneaster
Cytisus	Elderflower	Fig	Forsythia	Grasses
Hawthorn	Honeysuckle	Humulus	Ivy	Jasmine
Juniper	Kniphofia	Lavatera	Monarda	Papaver
Passiflora	Perovskia	Pyracantha	Tamarix	Willow

Both Clematis and Rhododendron grow quickly.

Floppers and smotherers

Actinidia	*Akebia*	*Asparagus*	*Campsis*	*Chrysanthemum*
Clematis	*Comfrey*	*Delphinium*	*Gladioli*	*Gunnera*
Hollyhock	*Humulus*	*Ivy*	*Passiflora*	*Persicaria*
Rhus	*Trachelospermum*	*Tropaeolum*	*Wisteria*	

Papaver have beautiful flowers but not so beautiful foliage, which always flops over.

Tulips, Ferns, Foxgloves, Geraniums, Lavender and Crocus are just wonderful plants.

146　　　　　　　　　I want to like my garden

Designing with 'boxes'

The plants below have been sorted into shape boxes, this is not the shape of the plant, it is the space it takes up; hence why small trees are an inverted pyramid, other plants are shaped more like a shoe box. Knowing the approximate size, the plant will want to grow to and the rough shape it uses in the border means borders can be planned with different shaped boxes. Not every plant is included here; just most of the plants that are sold in most garden centres and plant nurseries and the colours they come in.

Small Tops & T Shirts

Smaller plant < 0.5m x 0.5m

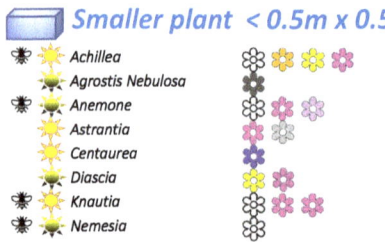

Achillea	This is just a really good plant, it goes with everything
Agrostis Nebulosa	Known as cloud grass which froths round other plants
Anemone	A spring bulb best popped under trees
Astrantia	Best in sun will flower in light shade
Centaurea	Best in poor soil, use more natural looking flower shapes
Diascia	Use more natural coloured varieties or they can look a bit false
Knautia	Flowers like pincushions, hates soggy heavy soils
Nemesia	Really pretty, but needs winter protection, is best grown in a pot

Skinny plant <1m tall

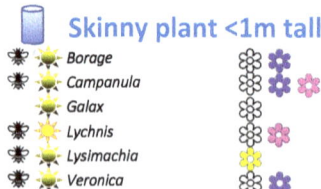

Borage	A self seed expert, a bit untidy but great for bees and Pimms
Campanula	The nicest ones are tall and thin; simple flowers look the best
Galax	Cool shady spot and white flowers
Lychnis	Lychnis Coronaria self seeds everywhere; but is lovely!
Lysimachia	Not for a formal garden border, it needs wet soil
Veronica	Will need splitting every few years to stop it flopping

Useful stuff to know about plants 147

Small Jeans & Petit Jumpers

Thin Plant < 1m tall

	Digitalis		Foxgloves, there's nothing not to like about them
	Dill		Will self-seed everywhere, but is a very tactile plant
	Dryopteris		Tall green fern that requires no looking after, grows in deep dry shade too
	Eryngium		A bit spiky, but is beloved by bees and butterflies
	Ferns		The only place ferns hate growing in is a hot sunny dry baked place
	Millium		A shade loving grass in bright yellow; hurrah!
	Verbascum		Furry silvery leaves, tall spikes, needs staking; you either love them or don't

Low growing spreader < 0.5m tall

	Bergenia		Grows in the toughest places with big elephant ear shaped shiny leaves
	Brunnera		Grows in tough spots is perfect for planting around shrub bases
	Convolvulus		This is a brilliant plant for hot sunny sites with poor soil
	Erigeron		Will grow everywhere, a prolific self-seeder; but it's pretty so who cares!
	Galium		Will spread and be a carpet under plants and shrubs, but it will spread!
	Imperata Rubra		For those who want grass that's not green; this is red
	Libertia		This will hate soggy boggy places but is a great plant; very well behaved
	Ophiopogon		Is very shallow rooted so easy to pull up in error
	Potentilla		Looks a bit like a mini rose, without thorns or blackspot
	Sagina		Another carpet mat of a plant, hates soggy bottoms
	Stachys		Planted mainly for it's silvery leaf colour - but needs sunshine
	Thymus		Who would not like thyme?

Smaller plant < 0.5m x 0.5m

	Amsonia		A useful 'goes with anything' kind of plant
	Calluna		Needs an open site and acid soil or don't bother growing it
	Carex		A useful 'goes with anything' kind of plant
	Elymus		It's a bit shaggy, but it's the best blue grass there is
	Erica		Needs an open site and acid soil or don't bother growing it
	Gypsophilia		One of the best plants to stuff everywhere in a sunny border
	Geum		Just a self sufficient, goes with anything, happy plant
	Hakenochloa		A yellow grass that forms carpets under trees
	Hellebore		For something that flowers in the winter, but cut off old foliage
	Heuchera		All shades of foliage colour and flowers, the bees love
	Hosta		Amazing leaves but beloved by slugs and snails

Mid-Sized Top & T Shirts

🪣 Grows < 1.5m tall but upright

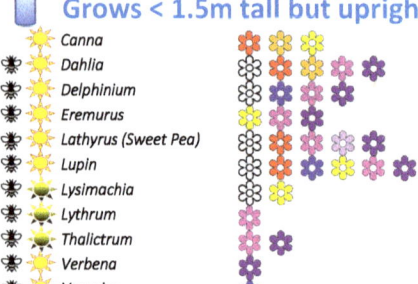

	Canna	A tropical looking plant, needs a rich soil and no drought
	Dahlia	Dahlias require gardening effort to grow well and look amazing
	Delphinium	Delphiniums are for those who are avid gardeners
	Eremurus	One for a gardener who wants to be noticed
	Lathyrus (Sweet Pea)	The only reason you grow them is for the scent
	Lupin	Everyone loves a Lupin, but so do Aphids!
	Lysimachia	Tall thin spires of white or yellow flowers
	Lythrum	These are best grown on wet ground
	Thalictrum	Will fall over and disappears in winter, but is a stunner in summer
	Verbena	A scratchy stemmed plant but essential for any garden
	Veronica	Just as nice as a Delphinium but easier to grow

🧱 Medium plant up to 1m x 1m

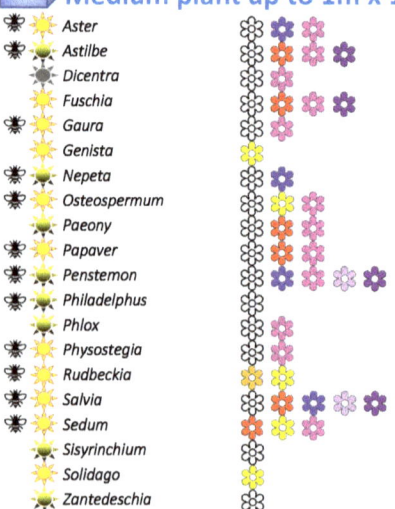

	Aster	A happy daisy like flower for later in the year
	Astilbe	A bit like Marmite, you love them or hate them!
	Dicentra	Lovely foliage, pretty flowers, loves dappled shade
	Fuschia	Boring shrubs until they flower
	Gaura	May not last too long, is a bit floppy but oh so lovely
	Genista	For lovers of sunshine yellow flowers
	Nepeta	These can be a bit untidy, but smell lovely
	Osteospermum	A happy daisy flower, hates cold cold soggy soil
	Paeony	Everyone should have paeonies in the garden
	Papaver	Poppy flowers are stunning but shortlived, foliage is messy
	Penstemon	Very pretty plant in lots of colours and sizes
	Philadelphus	Amazing scent, but fast growing and untidy, get the smaller variety
	Phlox	Get the taller varieties, not the alpine plants (too twee)
	Physostegia	Loads to choose from but buy a perennial not an annual
	Rudbeckia	Will spread and form a mat, but is easily 'refereed'
	Salvia	Late summer feel good happy flowers; needs to be bulk planted
	Sedum	Goes with anything type of plant but needs good drainage
	Sisyrinchium	Goes with anything type of plant
	Solidago	Called Goldenrods, plant in groups not singly
	Zantedeschia	Prefers a damper spot and best planted en masse

Useful stuff to know about plants   149

Under 0.5m tall but spreads wider

☀	Agastache		Smells of aniseed; grow in a warm sheltered spot
☀	Ajuga		Covers shady areas in leaves and pretty blue flowers
	Alchemilla		Great leaves but will spread everywhere
	Coreopsis		Poor soil and lots of sun = lots of flowers
☀	Pulmonaria		A plant used more for it's foliage than it's flowers
☀	Ranunculus		A type of buttercup and the best colour for buttercups is yellow
☀	Thymus		Thyme, a fantastic plant for bees
☀	Valerian		A grows anywhere kind of plant, but pretty

Mid-Sized Jeans & Jumpers

Larger plants up to 2m x 2m

☀	Abelia		Very pretty, very fragrant but can get pretty tall and a bit untidy
	Aucuba		A well behaved shrub that will grow anywhere (but doesn't do much)
	Berberis		Red green or almost black foliage, but it has really big thorns
	Camellia		Dull green shrub with glossy leaves and rather plastic looking flowers
☀	Choisya		A well behaved smaller shrub in yellow
☀	Cimicifuga		Some don't like the smell, but the flowers are great
☀	Cornus		Boring with leaves on, amazing stem colour in winter. Needs pruning
☀	Crambe Cordifolia		Slugs and snails love the leaves, employ a toad or hedgehog to help
☀	Daphne		Just has the best 'spring is here' scent ever
☀	Deutzia		A happy plant with happy flowers
	Hydrangeu		Hydra means water, these have big flowers which need lots of water
☀	Leucanthemum		Hates bone dry soils, but will be a happy flower in light shade too
☀	Olearia		Tough, fast growing, can be prickly. Use it as a wind protector
☀	Philadelphus		Fast growing, untidy shape but lovely scent. Needs really proper pruning
	Pieris		White flowers, red leaves. An alternative to a green shrub
☀	Roses		Always requires proper pruning which is a pain as the thorns hurt!
	Sanguisorba		A floppy plant but fun, lots of pink drumsticks wave in the air
☀	Skimmia		Fabulous shrub, smells amazing, bees love it and is very well behaved
	Weigela		Bit dull, bit boring but will grow and flower in a shady spot

Wider at the top but < 2m tall

	Callicarpa		Stunning metallic berries (that the birds quickly eat) Hates cold soggy roots
☀	Callistemon		Needs proper pruning or you don't get enough flowers
	Hibiscus		Showy but short lived flowering season. Prone to aphid attack
	Kolkwitzia		Tall floppy but pretty
	Miscanthus		A tall elegant grass, don't stuff it in a corner, it needs space to look nice
☀	Perovskia		It must have the 'chelsea chop' or it flops, so don't forget
	Poa		A green grass best in a tall pot. Don't plant in manure rich compost

Medium plant up to 1m x 1m

	Acanthus		Unusual plant, slightly prickly leaves, weird looking flowers
	Agapanthus		Needs warm sun and really sharp drainage. Will spread itself about
	Alstromeria		Will spread wide, some flowers look too artificially coloured though
	Artemesia		Used as a foliage plant. Will hate soggy wet soil in winter
	Aster		Happy autumn flowering daisies; enough said
	Buxus		A green bush you can shape into anything
	Cistus		If you want lots of flowers, keep deadheading
	Cytisus		An untidy plant with yellow flowers
	Echinacea		Late summer flowering daisy shaped flowers, it's a very happy flower
	Hebe		All shapes all sizes, some need regular pruning some won't
	Kniphofia		Unusual flowers but an untidy looking plant
	Lavender		If you don't prune lavender properly it gets untidy
	Ligularia		You will fight the slugs and snails, but it is a nice plant
	Monarda		Bee Balm, but without a moist soil it can look a bit 'off colour'
	Myrtus		A bit like buxus but with white flowers, hates cold wet soil
	Phormium		Ternax is the variety to avoid, it gets huge
	Rosemary		Beloved by bees and lamb chops
	Sarcococca		Every garden must have space for one of these plants

Shorter but spreads up to 1m wide

	Caltha		One for the soggy bottoms here. Wet soil and dappled shade = happier flowers
	Euphorbia		Handle with gloves on, the sap is an irritant.
	Geranium		All sizes, all shapes, make sure the one you choose fits the space you have
	Helenium		Won't flower well in really dry soils. Not for hayfever sufferers
	Helianthemum		Can look a bit twee, it will not survive a soggy bottom all winter
	Hemerocallis		Day lily, lots of flowers lasting one day each, but it's a bit untidy
	Kerria		Doesn't like cold exposed places, not a plant to use as a show stopper
	Mertensia		Not terribly exciting, not very showy but good in a shady spot
	Nepeta		Can look a little like a bad hair day especially if the cat's rolled in it!
	Pennisetum		One of the best touchy-feely grasses. Some aren't terrible hardy though
	Rue		A plant with blue leaves, which is why you have it. It can irritate the skin

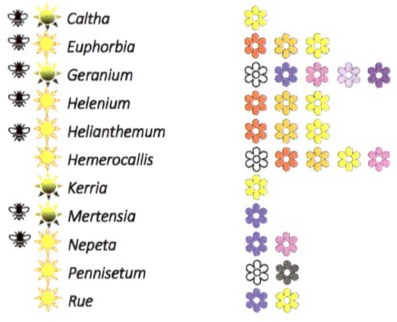

Useful stuff to know about plants 151

Large Jeans & Oversized Jumpers

Big plants that take up more than 2m

	Abutilon		Dusty foliage that makes you sneeze, but it is pretty. Is a fast grower
	Acer		Hates full sun and drying winds which shrivel the leaves
	Amelanchier		Grown for its spring flowers & autumn foliage but it can get untidy looking
	Buddleja		Will quickly disappoint if not pruned properly
	Lavatera		Fast growing plants with saucer shaped flowers, they can look untidy though
	Magnolia		These take up a lot of space in the garden but they are stunning
	Salix		Are really fast growing, neglect the pruning at your peril
	Sambucus		Colourful foliage but produces black berries which means purple bird poo!
	Sophora		It's different and has stunning yellow flowers, but won't like cold wet winters
	Syringa		If you want the flowers where you can smell them, it needs proper pruning

More than 1m wide

	Chrysanthemum		Can be amazing, can also look like a plant that's had lots of cosmetic surgery
	Crocosmia		Is a lovely plant in any garden, but can spread itself about too much
	Hypericum		One for a tough spot, not for a pretty place in the garden
	Ligustrum		Privet, a bit like structural underwear, essential but a bit boring
	Persicaria		Plant it by itself, it will outcompete all other plants, but is great for bees

Really large plant over 2m x 2m

	Ceanothus		A bit of a boring shrub until it flowers
	Cotinus Coggyria		Only plant where the sun can shine through the leaves which is the best bit
	Cotoneaster		This is an untidy scraggy looking shrub with nice red berries, if you like berries
	Eleagnus		A shrub to be used as background plant only
	Escallonia		It flowers pink in the spring, will become impenetrable if left
	Euonymous		A shrub to be used as background plant only
	Griselinia		If you need an attractive big green shrub; this is the one
	Fatsia		Will regrow easily if you cut branches out, great shaped leaves
	Forsythia		A really boring and untidy shrub until it flowers
	Fothergilla		Another boring shrub until it flowers
	Mahonia		Prickly leaves, don't plant near a path, but amazing scent in winter
	Osmanthus		Dark green leaves, a bit boring but it does have fragrant white flowers
	Photinia		Gets too big too quickly and has red leaves (have a Cotinus instead)
	Pittosporum		If you need a big boring shrub, at least have a pretty big boring shrub
	Rhododendron		All shapes, all sizes, just make sure it fits the space you have available
	Viburnum		A lightsucking green leaved shrub that redeems itself in winter

Tall plants over 1-2m tall or climbers

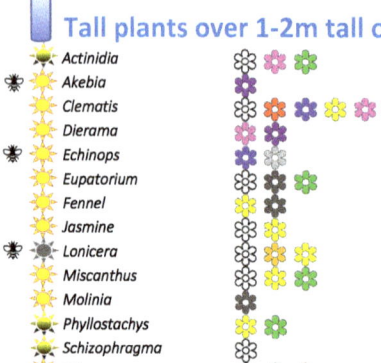

Actinidia		A climber that has multi coloured leaves/flowers
Akebia		This grows fast and gets big, but is very pretty
Clematis		Cool roots and sunny tops needed. Always plant Clematis deep down in the soil
Dierama		Hates being moved. Not near paths, the leaves are long and trippy-uppy
Echinops		A bit prickly, will bulk up quickly, can topple over, but brilliant for watching bees
Eupatorium		Only appears late summer and autumn, flowers like mad and then dies down again
Fennel		Self- seeds everywhere, it also has massive tap root that's difficult to dig out
Jasmine		Smells lovely but is a messy untidy climber
Lonicera		Smells lovely, is a really untidy climber, it needs proper pruning to perform
Miscanthus		A tall but undemanding attractive grass.
Molinia		The base can look bit messy, don't surround it with any big tall plants
Phyllostachys		Strong winds and sunshine = lots of shredded leaves. Canes will need thinning out
Schizophragma		A shade loving self clinging climber, it will spread and root along the ground too
Stipa		Needs sun and space and not being surrounded by other tall plants
Wisteria		Will only look stunning if properly pruned, it gets very big and heavy

Useful stuff to know about plants

Accessories

Flowers in month

Plant	Months	Description
Galanthus	2-3	These are Snowdrops
Ammi Majus	2-3	This is a posh Cow Parsley
Anemone Blanda	2-3	A ground covering daisy like flower, that's very pretty
Aquilegia	2-3	Has soft pretty foliage and flowers, but it does self seed, a lot
Celandine	2-3	A happy smiling 'spring is here' plant with buttercup yellow flowers
Crocus	2-3	NB: The birds prefer eating the yellow ones
Daffodil	2-3	Come in all colours of yellow, white and orange!
Muscari	2-3	Also known as the Grape Hyacinth
Narcissus	2-3	A prettier Daffodil
Primula	3-4	Are Primrose, the nicest colour is always yellow
Allium	4-5	Every garden should have Alliums
Anthriscus	4-5	Another posh Cow Parsley
Bluebell	4-5	English Bluebells have nodding flowers heads, only use these ones.
Galium	4-5	Sweet Woodruff, a ground covering really pretty plant
Iris	4-6	Iris comes in every colour, except a really bright red
Myosotis	4-5	Forget Me Not, is very pretty but very prolific
Tulip	4-5	Who does not love Tulips?
Alyssum	4-6	This is a carpet forming plant with oodles of flowers
Armeria	5-6	Think green cushion with lollipop sticks of flowers on top
Aubretia	5-6	A bit like Alyssum and comes in different colours
Camassia	5-6	Bright blue bulbs that pop up, flower and disappear again
Convallaria	5-6	Lily of the Valley, is highly scented but it will spread
Fritilleria	5-6	A tall Lily like flower, but beloved by lily beetles too
Orlaya	5-6	A summer flowering posh cow parsley
Ornithogalum	5-6	A shade loving bulb sprouting starry white flowers
Catananche	6-8	A star shaped thin papery flower
Circium	6-8	Posh thistles, but still prickly
Cosmos	6-8	A 'make you smile' plant with soft foliage and happy flowers
Cyclamen	6-8	Low growing sending up flowers before any leaves grow
Dianthus	6-8	Has lovely silvery foliage, but some can look a bit fake
Diascia	6-8	Some of the flowers can be a bit too sugary pink
Emilia	6-8	Has a flower that looks like a tiny paint brush
Escholitzia	6-8	A really happy 'I love sunbathing' flower
Gentian	6-8	A blue flower for lovers of blue
Gladioli	6-8	Some are awful looking garish flowers but some aren't
Lily	6-8	Wonderful flowers if you can stop the lily beetle eating them!
Scabiosa	6-8	A pincushion shaped flower beloved by bees and butterflies
Dahlia	7-10	Some are great and some are ghoulish
Deschampsia	7-10	A frothy cloud grass, adds a soft focus to most borders
Schizostylis	8-11	A lily like flower that erupts in October
Viola	10-11	Dainty and pretty but can have rather garish colours

- Really loved by bees and butterflies
- Most common flower or leaf colour available
- For best results grow this in a sunny spot
- Will still perform well in light shade
- Is happy growing in shaded spots

All plants listed are commonly available in garden centres or nurseries
Most annual bedding is not listed, neither are trees or plants unsuitable for small gardens
The colours shown relate to the most commonly sold varieties
The sizes shown relates to the most commonly sold varieties

Bibliography

Readers Digest. (2003). *New Encyclopaedia of Garden Plants & Flowers.* London. Readers Digest.

Ferguson, Nicola. (1996). *Right Plant Right Place.* UK. Aura Books plc.

Royal Horticultural Society website: sourced information

https://www.rhs.org.uk/Plants/18969/i-Vinca-major-i/Details

Useful Websites

Plant nurseries:

crocus.co.uk,
knollsgardens.co.uk,
meadowmania.co.uk,
nurseriesonline.co.uk

primrose.co.uk,
seedbombs.co.uk
wildflowers.co.uk
wildseed.co.uk

Garden advice:

rhs.org.uk
plantplots.com (sorry, I had to give my website a plug!)

Conservation:

hotbincomposting.com
bokashidirect.co.uk
butterfly-conservation.org

hedgehogcare.org
mothscount.org

Ethical garden supplies:

bluepatch.org
ethicalsuperstore.com

greenshop.co.uk

Rachel McCartain does not endorse or recommend any particular products or services; the above listings are provided for information purposes only.

Index

Avoiding Mistakes
  Centrifuge planting, *84*
  Do something, *86*
  Faking nature, *86*
  Creating a balanced border, *87*
  Don't hide a problem, *88*
  Patios need to be bigger than you think, *89*
  Poorly designed paths, *90*
  Hiding behind a big green wall, *94*
  Trellis troubles, *96*
  Dead space, *99*
  Hanging baskets, *100*
  Getting the lawn wrong, *103*
  Making a mess of a mulch, *106*
  Power tools can't prune, *107*
  Salt & pepper planting styles, *109*
  Small spaces don't need small plants, *109*
  The downside of vegetable gardens, *111*

Be a Better Gardener
  By gardening less, *113*
  Buying the wrong sort of plants, *115*
  Plants aren't always environmentally friendly, *117*
  How insect friendly are the plants you buy?, *122*
  BEE more friendly, *124*
  Show gardens are just that, they are a show!, *125*
  Gardens ARE part of nature, *126*
  Buy what you need, not what you want, *129*
  It's your garden not anyone else's, *131*
Boring gardens aren't designed they evolve, *16*

Chelsea Chop, *43*
Chemical sprays, *46*, *83*, *94*, *114*, *134*
Common Garden Mistakes, *84*

Contemporary or Modern Gardens, *80*
Cottage gardens, *80*
Courtyard Spaces:, *65*
Creating a Design
  Starting the process, *64*
  Doing the drawing. *70*
  Fitting it all together, *73*
  Planning the planting, *74*
  Designing with boxes, *76*

Design Ideas
  Front gardens, *23*
  Back gardens, *25*
  Lawns, *71*
  Seating areas, *72*
  Where should a path go?, *72*
  Storing stuff, *72*
  How do you plan what to plant?, *74*
  Using box shapes to plan the planting, *76*
  Mediterranean gardens, *79*
  Cottage gardens, *80*
  Contemporary / modern gardens, *80*
  Exotic gardens styles, *81*
  Natural or eco-friendly gardens, *82*
Design Rules
  What is the regulatory line?, *52*
  One thirds rule, *53*
  Garden symmetry, *54*
  The golden ratio, *55*
  It's your garden!, *56*
  Don't create unnecessary work, *57*
  Designing around immovable eyesores, *58*
  Paths, get them right, *92*
Designing with boxes
  Small tops and T shirts, *146*
  Small jeans and jumpers, *147*
  Medium tops and T shirts, *148*
  Medium jeans and jumpers, *149*
  Large jeans and jumpers, *151*
  Accessories, *153*

Index

DO YOU LIKE YOUR GARDEN?, *5*

Effort to Reward ratio, *16*
Emotions - gardens should feel good, *6*
Environmental problems, *6*
Exotic gardens, *81*

First time gardeners, *63*

Garden Skills like pruning, *2*
Garden Wardrobe, *138*
Gardening, what actually is it?, *2*
Gardens
    Falling back in love with your garden, *20*
    How to put things right again, *16*
    Simple changes create a whole new garden, *18*
    Front gardens, *23*
    Back gardens, *25*
    Why gardens 'fail', *6*
Garlic spray recipe, *134*

Hints & Tips
    Before you buy any plants, *12*
    Reworking the wardrobe, *19*
    Learning to love the garden more, *21*
    Time-consuming chores, *30*
    Easier shrubs, *31*
    Easier climbers, *31*
    Easier plants, *32*
    Easier pots, *32*
    Easier weedingl, *33*
    Planting advice, *35*
    Planting larger plants, *35*
    Why plants in pots die, *36*
    Stopping the flopping, *42*
    Dealing with bugs, *46*
    Designing in a really small garden, *67*
    Deciding what to plant, *77*
    Lawn, *105*
    Sticking to a planting plan, *109*
    Smart planting for small spaces, *110*
    Garden centres, plant nursery or DIY store?, *116*
    Buying plants for the first time, *119*

How to attract bees & butterflies, *124*
HOW TO CHANGE THE GARDEN, *50*
HOW YOUR GARDEN CAN HELP SAVE THE WORLD, *113*
    Privacy, *67*, *68*, *94*, *95*

IMPROVING THE GARDEN, *22*
Invasion of the garden dome, *108*

Low maintenance borders, *33*
Low maintenance climbers, *31*
Low maintenance plants, *32*
Low maintenance pots, *32*
Low maintenance shrubs, *31*
Lower maintenance gardens, *26*

Manhole Covers or Drains, *58*
Maximising space, *51*
Mediterranean gardens, *79*
Messy gardens, planning for debris, *14*

Natural (Eco-friendly) Gardens, *82*

OK IT MIGHT NOT BE THE WORLDS GREATEST GARDEN BUT…, *130*
Outside 'rooms', *80*

Perfectly good pruning, *38*
Planting a problem, *10*
Plants
    Aren't always good for the garden, *13*
    Change creates interest, *18*
    Choose plants by how they make you feel, *10*
    Connecting you to your garden, *9*
    Happy plants don't misbehave, *11*
    'Instant' gardens rarely work, *11*
    Plan for debris, *14*
Pruning, *38*

Rules to Remember
    Front gardens, *23*
    Proper planting, *34*
    Planting in pots, *37*
    Pruning, *41*

Index

Before you change anything!, *52*
The 80/20 Rule, *69*
Paths and pathways, *91*
Lawns, *105*
Sacrificial plants, *47*
Senses Test, *120*
Sheds, *58*, *59*, *73*, *74*, *88*
Size in Five, *120*
Structural problems, *6*

Tables
  Garden wardrobe, *19*
  Trellis, *97*
  Garden centre or plant nursery?, *117*
  Plant labels and what they really mean, *121*
  Needy vegetables, *133*
  Plants that fight back, *135*
  Creating your own wardrobe, *138*
  Plants that won't flop over, *139*
  'Look at me!' plants, *139*
  Loud and proud flowers, *140*
  Cooler coloured flowers, *140*
  Plants to touch, *141*
  Happy flowers, *141*
  Plants that aren't green, *142*
  Plants that dance in the breeze, *142*
  Scented plants, *142*
  Every garden should have these plants, *142*
  Messy trees and untidy plants, *143*
  Fast growing plants, *143*
  Plants that never look tidy, *143*
Time consuming chores, *29*
Trowel Test, *34*

Urban gardens, *54*
USEFUL STUFF TO KNOW ABOUT PLANTS, *132*

Vegetable gardens, *111*

Weeding, *30*, *45*
What goes wrong
  Why can't you enjoy the garden?, *6*
  Wrong plant, wrong place, *27*
  Overfilling borders, *28*
  Plants that get too big, *40*
  Limp or threadbare looking plants, *41*
  The plants flop over, *42*
  Unwanted plants, *43*
  Plants that take over the garden, *44*
  Weeds, they're everywhere!, *45*
  Plant munching bugs, *46*
  Lousy looking lawns, *48*
  Over ambition, *63*

And finally ...

I hope that having read this book you now feel more ready to tackle your garden and create a place you truly enjoy being in. Do please post your before and after pictures on our Facebook page facebook.com/PlantPlots – we would all really love to see them!

You can also email your pictures and I will add them to the PlantPlots 'Gallery of Gorgeous Gardens'. Send any pictures to design@plantplots.com

If though you are still a bit stuck, do please get in touch, I have created designs for single garden borders or can remodel the whole garden, if you just want a bit of advice however, that is always free and given without obligation. You can find customer reviews of my design service via TrustPilot.com/review/PlantPlots.

Happy gardening!

Rachel

'Finding Rachel's website was the best thing I could have done and well worth the affordable fee, which was a lot lower than I expected.'

'Rachel of PlantPlots delivered above and beyond expectations – incredible value!'

'I found PlantPlots during a google search, I wasn't sure what to expect from a designer that doesn't come to your garden, but OMG Rachel is amazing,'

'It's a masterpiece!'

'We cannot recommend Rachel and the team's work more highly. Simply put, Rachel is a miracle worker and lovely person.'

PlantPlots.com

About the Author

Although never having any formal horticultural qualifications, Rachel grew up helping in her father's plant nursery. It was whilst shovelling half a tonne of rotten onion sets, she developed a near pathological hatred of gardening and vowed never to pursue a career in horticulture ever! Instead she attained a Business Studies Degree from Brighton and worked for BMW for several years before starting a family.

Subsequently, her antipathy toward gardening eroded away, having moved to a house whose garden was an unloved weed infested wilderness; transforming this mess into a practical and family friendly space gradually helped develop a love of gardening particularly in working out how to have a great looking garden whilst having to juggle all the other elements modern life brings.

In recent years, Rachel founded PlantPlots as an online garden design company, providing practical garden designs for customers who wanted a better-looking garden, but had no clue how to start. She has created designs in both the UK and the USA.

Rachel currently lives by the sea in West Sussex, UK, she is married with three children. Although having pets has never been high on her list of must haves, her garden does boast a chicken wire heron name Eric, a shoal of wire 'Michael' fish (named after a departed uncle) and in pride of place a seven-foot sunbathing topiary leopard called Ingwe. Rachel is currently planning whether to 'grow' a giraffe or some antelopes for Ingwe to hunt.

www.ingramcontent.com/pod-product-compliance
Lightning Source LLC
Chambersburg PA
CBHW060538100426
42743CB00009B/1568